John Adair

effective
teambuilding

HOW TO MAKE A WINNING TEAM

PAN BOOKS

First published 1986 by Gower Publishing Ltd

This edition published 1987 by Pan Books
an imprint of Pan Macmillan Ltd
Pan Macmillan, 20 New Wharf Road, London N1 9RR
Basingstoke and Oxford
Associated companies throughout the world
www.panmacmillan.com

ISBN 0 330 29809 7

20 19 18 17 16

A CIP catalogue record for this book is available from
the British Library.

Printed and bound in Great Britain by
Mackays of Chatham plc, Chatham, Kent

Contents

Introduction

Few things are more satisfying in life than belonging to a really successful team. There are few more rewarding activities than using your qualities and skills as a leader to create such a team.

The aim of this book is to help you to choose, build, maintain and lead teams at work.

Let us start by saying that a team is a group in which the individuals share a common aim and in which the jobs and skills of each member fit in with those of the others; and let us see if we find in the course of this book that other qualities are necessary or desirable.

As any good racing driver knows, the team who designed and built the car and the team who service it before, during and after the race are as necessary for success as he is himself. Generating effective team work is equally important in industry, commerce and the public services as it is in the world of professional sport, if not more so. How to get the right people in the team, how to get them to work together, how to raise their standards of performance; that in a nutshell is what this book is about.

Whether you are thinking primarily about your responsibilities as a leader or as a team member or – more likely – with *both* in mind, then you should carefully work through the checklists. They are designed to aid you to think and to apply the principles, lessons or rules of thumb to your own situation.

For this is essentially a practical book. When you have read and studied it in the light of your experience you should have most of the relevant knowledge about groups and teams you need. Then you must put it into practice.

Acknowledgements

May I thank most warmly John Armitt, Deputy Managing Director of John Laing International Ltd and Garth Ward, Project Manager of Bechtel Great Britain Ltd, for letting me quote extensively from their papers; and also the British Institute of Management, organisers of the conference at which the papers were given, for agreeing to let me publish extracts. I am also grateful to Bernard Babington Smith for reading the book in typescript and for making so many constructive suggestions. Lastly, I wish to thank again Jennifer Perraton for typing the drafts so competently, and Ellen Keeling for editing the subsequent proofs with her customary care and skill.

Part One
UNDERSTANDING GROUPS AND INDIVIDUALS

Like any craftsman a leader must first understand his raw material. Just as a wood carver learns to work with the grain so a leader must learn the nature of groups so that he can work *with* rather than *against* it.

To understand the phenomenon of groups I shall draw largely upon the tradition known as Group Dynamics. This phrase was coined by Kurt Lewin (1890-1947), the principal figure in the early days of the movement in America during the 1930s.

The term group dynamics came to be used in two different ways. In its most general and basic sense, it was – and still is – used to describe something that is happening in all groups at all times, whether anyone is aware of it or not. Group dynamics in this sense refers to the interacting forces within a small human group that cause it to behave the way it does.

The study by social psychologists and others of these forces – why groups behave the way they do – was also known as Group Dynamics, which gives us the second main sense of the word. That includes the findings of such studies, and the theorising that preceded or followed observation. Group Dynamics amounted to a movement, which is why I use capital letters for it in that context.

As a training method for large numbers of leaders, the Group Dynamics approach was too time-consuming.[1] Moreover, it was flawed by hidden assumptions of various kinds, such as those concerning leadership which I shall come to later. As a system of ideas or philosophy the movement reflected the preoccupations of American society and especially of humanist psychologists within it in the 1950s. Therefore, it was much more culture bound than its advocates were aware.

But like many ruins Group Dynamics makes a marvellous quarry for new builders. In writing Part One I have pictured myself walking around and over that collapsed edifice and selecting here and there a stone, a length of timber, a door or piece of ironwork which I feel can still be put to use. Alternatively, I see myself as one borrowing recipes from old cookbooks and adapting them in the light of my experience. Some of the materials remain the same; others have been transformed beyond recognition. But I can think of no better foundation to effective teambuilding than this piecing-together of an understanding of how human groups work, inspired by those remarkable pioneering efforts in America during the last half century.

1 Groups

Consider a queue waiting for a bus, a cluster of people having a drink together, a crowd of angry workers on strike and a rowing eight. Which of them could be termed a group?

It is difficult to say, isn't it? For *group* is a concept. Like many concepts, such as love or friendship, it is not susceptible to a single definition. It sounds more concrete than those abstract words, but it is just as hard to pin down. We all know what a group is – until we are asked!

In situations like this I usually resort to the dictionaries to try to discover the picture behind the general word. Group, which appears in French as *groupe* and Italian as *gruppo*, seems to be of German origin. It then meant: a cluster; a bunch or knot or bump; a heap; a bag (of money). These word pictures suggest a number of things or people together – no more than that.

SOME DEFINITIONS CONSIDERED

The value of the word *group* largely lies in its vagueness. The biologist, for example, can use it to describe an assemblage of

3

related organisms when he wishes to avoid taxonomic connotations, when the kind or degree of relationship is not clearly defined. Likewise the psychologist can employ it for a number of persons when he does not wish to be – or cannot be – too specific about their relation or degree of similarity. Edgar H.Schein[2] does not take us much further when he offers this definition:

A psychological group is any number of people who (1) interact with one another, (2) are psychologically aware of one another, and (3) perceive themselves to be a group.

The size of the group is therefore limited by the possibilities of mutual interaction and mutual awareness. At least this definition also rules out mere aggregates of people, like the crowd waiting for a train on a station platform or passengers sitting together in an airliner. Work teams, committees and cliques would fall within its boundaries.

There are many variations on the themes above. Bernard M. Bass[3], to give another instance, defined a group as

A collection of individuals whose existence as a collection is rewarding to the individuals (or enables them to avoid punishment). A group does not necessarily perceive itself as such. The members do not have to share common goals. Nor are interaction, interlocking roles, and shared ways of behaviour implied in the definition, although these are common characteristics of many groups.

You will notice the points of disagreement between Schein's and Bass's definitions. Do groups perceive themselves as such? Is interaction intrinsic to them?

These examples – and disagreements – could be multiplied. They take us back to the points that *group* is a general word and that part of its attraction is that it can be used when the factors mentioned above are either not known to be present or are not clearly defined.

For precision of a language, Karl Popper has pointed out, depends upon not burdening its terms with the task of being precise. The terms 'sand dune' and 'wind' are vague, yet for many geological purposes they are sufficiently precise. Besides, we can always qualify them, if necessary. The notion that precise knowledge requires precise definition is wrong.

We operate with concepts such as 'energy' and 'light', which are not capable of being reduced to a simple definition. So it is with 'group'.

WORK GROUPS

Things are more precise if we do introduce a broad qualification and focus upon groups found in work environments – in a design office, purchasing section, night shift or executive committee. Here, for example, there is a very high probability that there will be some sort of common task. Such work groups are deep-rooted; they are part of the primary social experience for mankind. In the mists of prehistory we can imagine a group of men banding together to hunt a hairy mammoth. Perhaps some dig a pit and cover the top with branches while others locate the prey and drive it towards the trap. After the kill they divide up the meat in some order of status and take the spoils home to their cave dwellings.

It is not too fanciful to trace the descent of all working groups – expedition armies, business enterprises – from that ancestor, the primitive hunting group.

The other primary group is of course the *family*. It is instructive to consider some of the differences between work groups and families – this is shown in Fig. 1.1.

Work groups	*Families*
Have a common task (or a set of individual tasks) which tends to be explicit.	Serve two ends: companionship and the procreation and nurture of children. These are natural and often implicit.
Relationships are functional.	Relationships of parents and children are ontological.
Groups exist to work on tasks.	Families may tackle tasks, e.g. gardening together, but they are expressive rather than intrinsic to the family.

Leadership tends to go with competence. A young man may lead the hunting band.	Leadership traditionally tends to go with gender and seniority. Father is in charge.
Work groups are often temporary.	Family implies a much greater degree of permanence.

Fig. 1.1 Work Groups and Families

If the *work* qualification is introduced then many of the disagreements and differences of emphasis among psychologists about what distinguishes those collections of individuals that are groups from those that are not begin to fade. A collection of people is clearly a work group when it possesses most if not all of these characteristics:

- A definable membership – a collection of two or more people identifiable by name or type

- Group consciousness – the members think of themselves as a group, have a collective perception of unity, a conscious identification with each other

- A sense of shared purpose – the members have the same common task or goals or interests

- Interdependence – the members need the help of one another to accomplish the purposes for which they joined the group

- Interaction – the members communicate with one another, influence one another, react to one another

- Ability to act in a unitary manner – the group can work as a single organism

These factors can be pictured in a model, as below.

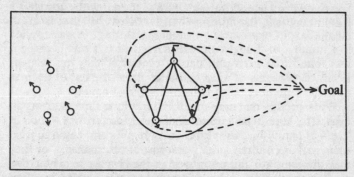

Fig. 1.2   Individuals and Groups

The individuals on the left hand of the diagram share no common goal. The goal arrows of the various individuals are centrifugal in this case. They lack a boundary, indicating a low consciousness of being a group and an ill-defined membership. No lines of interaction or interdependence link individuals. Clearly such a 'group' is unable to act as a whole.

Let us return to the differences between work groups and families. These should not be allowed to obscure the considerable overlap between them. Work groups, for example, can provide a considerable degree of mutual support and comfort. Companionship – a word directly related to *company* – is certainly experienced in organisations.

In both kinds of group, individuals acquire or shape their existing values and attitudes, beliefs and opinions, goals and ideals. The family is much more potent in this respect because a young child is more impressionable. School, which is a bridge between family and working life, comes next in potency, with the work groups we enter in young adult life, last. The attitudes we acquire in adult life are written in sand but the values accepted in childhood are engraved in stone.

Some families, of course, are also work groups. Most of us have watched a family of trapeze artists soaring through the air. There are family businesses which have begun with a father-son, brother-brother or husband-wife partnership. There have been famous family work groups, like the celebrated Von Trapp Singers whose early story was told in *The Sound of Music*.

In this context it is worth reflecting on the origins of the word 'team'. The dominating image for us today is the sports team in football, baseball, hockey or cricket. But originally, in Anglo-Saxon, team meant a family, offspring. It was applied to a number of draught animals harnessed in a row because it was found that oxen pull better together if they are related. From those teams of oxen or horses came the use of team to describe a number of persons in concerted action.

Work groups that stay together for a long time, such as an orchestra, tend to take on some of the characteristics – good or bad – of family life. Employers may regress and begin to treat their staff as children – the worst sort of paternalism – or they may develop into 'father-figures' in the best sense. The crews of British nuclear submarines today often refer to their captains as 'father'. The regiment and the business company, both institutions as well as organisations, conceive themselves as families. As a sergeant said to a bewildered young recruit, 'I am your mother now'. A fellow officer is called a 'brother officer'. It is more than analogy.

The case of the returning shop steward

Vic Fellows was a militant senior shop steward in the Chemical Division of a large British-owned multinational. In this capacity he frequently clashed with the Divisional Chairman, David Mellors. Eventually Fellows emigrated to Australia and the management heaved a sigh of relief. But things did not work out well for Fellows. His wife died after five years and five years later he lost his job through compulsory redundancy. With four children to support he wrote to Mellors, now Company Chairman, asking in desperation if he could come back. 'Of course I said yes', Mellors told me. 'He is one of the family'.

There can certainly be transfer of learning between these two fundamental kinds of group – in both directions. One study, for instance, suggested that people who find their work boring do not tend to compensate with interesting hobbies or activities in their spare time, as some sociologists – in order to defend the morality of giving people inhuman jobs and paying them well to do it – had suggested they would do so. Jobs which consist of drudgery or toil should be mechanised or automated, until we are left with an irreducible minimum of them. People should be paid exceptionally well to undertake them.

The family is also potentially a matrix for learning both social and rudimentary business skills, a point that is often overlooked. Consider this 1985 press report.

The hand that rocks the cradle

It is still harder for a woman in Britain to get financial backing to start her own business. In the United States 32 per cent of all businesses (the vast majority of which are small) are owned by women. In Britain, where trends lag some ten to fifteen years behind, the proportion is estimated at 6 to 8 per cent and rising. The barriers are falling away as women are proving particularly adept at running small businesses.

Management and business experts who are helping many of them to acquire the know-how to develop their enterprises say most housewives already possess the kind of skills they need. 'Anyone who has run a home, brought up children, entertained, mediated between the different requirements of the family members and catered to their needs already has the skills it takes to run a small business – or a bigger one for that matter', said one.

'The trouble is that society does not recognise and reward these skills so women do not realise they have them'.

Often women who have typically feminine qualities do not impress bank managers, while those who are aggressive or super-efficient put them off for the opposite reasons. Either way, women often can't win.

While the world's deeply-ingrained attitude to women is one obstacle, women's deeply-ingrained lack of confidence in themselves is yet another. Many get good, sometimes brilliant ideas: 'but I couldn't possibly do it' is the next thought. Men have no such inhibitions.

One study based on comparisons of 50 small-businesswomen with 50 small-businessmen, showed that the women usually had no managerial experience, while many men had, and often none of the technical or productive experience needed to create the products they were selling. Yet that did not stop them from being more successful.

Women have a wealth of creative and entrepreneurial ideas. Moreover, having been shaped outside the traditions of male business thinking, they tend to have fresh and unpredictable ways of making a business work. Since they often need to keep their business small, they grow slowly and surely, rather than getting out of control.

This could deprive some of the chance to make millions. But many women, with children's school timetables and households to think of, prefer – as one put it – 'to run it, rather than have it run me'.

And most women, unlike men, do not feel they have to live up to an image of success by, say, buying a Rolls-Royce. They tend to take less out of the business for themselves and invest more in making it work.

ORGANISATIONS AND COMMUNITIES

Some psychologists distinguish between:

Primary groups   Small numbers of individuals in regular face-to-face contact

Secondary groups Relatively large numbers – no-one has a clear picture of the other members

In working life an important instance of a larger secondary group is what we call an *organisation*. It is best to think of organisations as extensions of work groups. They are larger than small groups, although at what point one shades into the other is a matter for discussion.

An organisation is an association or body with an administrative and functional structure. It implies *systematic arrangement for a definite purpose*. That element of purpose is what relates it to its distant source in the hunting group and to its much nearer ancestor – the armies of the ancient world.

Institution is often used as a synonym for organisation. An institution, after all, is an establishment or society *instituted* for the promotion of some object – one of a public utility, religious, charitable, educational or other nature.

To me, however, institution carries a greater overtone of permanence. We can detect here the outlines of a familiar life-cycle. Many small *work groups* grow into *organisations*, which in turn become *institutions*. Not all organisations are institutions, but most are.

As a rule of thumb you can define an institution by whether or not it makes provision for paying pensions. Does it have methods of selecting and releasing people – a regular inflow and outflow of individuals – while retaining its essential character and continuing purpose?

The word organisation is related to organism, which reminds us that a root analogy for an organised *body* is the human body. Central to that metaphor is the concept of interdependence, that 'we are members one of another'.

From this image comes our most common metaphor for the leader – the *head* of the company, the *head* master or mistress, the *head* waiter, and so on.

By comparison *community* is more like an extension in numbers of the family: it is a tribal or kinship grouping. It suggests a unified body of people living in a common area of land. Local communities in turn belong to the wider community of a nation or state who share both common characteristics and a number of common political, social and religious institutions that have evolved over the centuries.

Not long ago the then Chairman of one of Britain's largest

nationalised industries spoke of it as a community. Is that right? Yes, because a community is any group of people with a common characteristic or interest living together within a larger society. The drawback of the word in this context is that it lies rather more in the *family* camp than in the *work group* camp. It may be better to think of such an industry as an *organisation* with a definite purpose to achieve rather than as a *community* sharing a common history and character, and common interests to promote or defend.

This may seem an academic point. But the long and damaging national coal strike in Britain (1984-5) hinged on the issue of whether or not the industry was an *organisation* there to produce coal at an economic rate for its customers, or a *community* composed of local mining communities which must at all costs be maintained, even regardless of the economic viability of the coal pits.

'Our pit was the mother of our community' said a striking miner on television in 1985. 'The pit is dead. What happens to our community?'

The *common interest* in any work community, no matter how long it has existed, must be in giving value for money in the service or goods it provides and thereby creating satisfied customers. If that becomes impossible then the *raison d'etre* of the industry – or that particular part of it – is gone. To maximise the chances of success calls for effective and efficient working together of all concerned: in a word, teamwork.

CHECKLIST: YOURSELF AS A GROUP MEMBER

- Think of the primary groups of which you are a member (work, social, family).

  Can you identify the needs in other group members fulfilled by their belonging to that group?

- Can you pick out some opinion, belief, value or goal which has been suggested to you, or shaped, by belonging to a group?

- What is the first small group (apart from your family) you belonged to? What were its characteristics?

- Do you contribute best in formal work groups, such as committees, or informal groups – those created by chance or as a result of personal preference?

- What three adjectives best describe your behaviour in most groups? How, in fact, do you see yourself *now* as a group member?

- What situation within groups cause you most problems? How do you handle them?
- What group skills would you like to develop? What strengths in behaviour in groups would you like to grow?

KEEP A DIARY

In order to write down your answers to these questions – an aid to clarity of thought – I suggest you use a stiff covered notebook. Keep it as a diary, adding ideas and insights, quotations and examples concerning teambuilding as they come to you. This book will give you some material, but you should be aware, while you are reading it, of other sources all around you. In this way you should be able to compile your own reference book on the subject, a sourcebook of knowledge, self-understanding, inspiration – and enjoyment – for years to come.

POINTS TO PONDER

Groups of both kinds – families and work groups – together with their larger counterparts, communities and organisations, are integral to human life.

The focus of this book is upon work groups. But you can apply many of its lessons in your family life or to the various social or community or church groups to which you might belong.

The starting point is for you to become more interested in, and more aware of, what is going on in groups. At the next group meeting you attend – preferably within two days of reading this chapter – resolve to sit and listen and observe as if you have never seen a group before in your life.

If you are not already aware of your chief personal strengths and weaknesses as a group member, ask two or three people who know you well to give you some constructive feedback.

Day by day you *can* become more effective in working groups. Keeping a diary of your steps in that direction over the next six months, together with key ideas from this book and elsewhere, and reviewing the contents from time to time, will help you immeasurably.

Groups are not only there to carry out tasks – they provide you with a series of unique opportunities to grow as a person.

2 Some properties of work groups

Work groups share certain properties with each other and with other kinds of group. There is such a profusion of them that the quest for similarities may seem a vain one. But it is possible to identify characteristics that all groups possess, albeit in varying degrees. These properties have received much attention from the researchers. They are of course overlapping and interactive, so it is better to regard them as facets of a single diamond than as separate entities.

In this chapter I shall outline a set of these properties. The list of them below is by no means exhaustive. Some of the properties, such as *common task*, *roles* and *leadership*, are reserved for later chapters, for instance, but cannot be divorced from the factors described in this chapter.

BACKGROUND

Each group has a historical background, or lack of it, which influences the way it behaves.

The members of a new group assembling for the first time may have to devote much of their energy at first to getting acquainted with one another, and deciding what needs to be done and how to do it. A well-established group, on the other hand, will be better acquainted with the situation. They may be assumed to know what to expect from each other and how to define the group's task. Ways of working together will have evolved. But such a group may also have developed habits that impair its effectiveness, such as unpunctuality, poor listening or wasting time.

Members come to a meeting of a new group or team with some expectations. They may have a clear idea of what it is about, or they may be uncertain about what is going to happen. They may be looking forward to being in that group or dreading it; they may feel deeply concerned or indifferent. In some cases the boundaries around the group's freedom of action may be tightly drawn by its terms of reference, or so poorly defined that the group doesn't know what its boundaries or limits are.

The history of the group in terms of its past successes and failures – its record in pursuing common objectives – is a central ingredient in background, relating as it does to group morale. Whether or not membership of the group in the past has been satisfying to each member is also another ingredient. The sense of sharing a common history – people, places and events – tends to bind people together. It gives them a dimension, a reference point, a depth, a quarry for memories and, often, a source of inspiration.

Most groups, especially those having relatively long histories, develop ceremonies and rituals, to help them cope with certain events, such as birthday celebrations, 'farewell drinks' when a member leaves the group, and 'initiation rites' of various kinds.

A crucial factor in group or team formation is therefore the amount of time that has been spent together. It takes time for a group personality to take shape. Nature does not work quickly. Relationships are as tender as plants when young but as strong as oaks when formed. If you want to build a team it is essential that you do get it together – and hold it together – over a significant period of time.

CHECKLIST

- What is the group's story so far? When did it come into being and for what purpose?

- Has the purpose of the group changed? If so, when did this occur and why?

- What is the composition of the group? What is the previous experience and personal history of each member? How were they related?

- What are the key experiences of success and failure which the group shares?

- What are the expectations of each member about the group and their role in it?

PARTICIPATION PATTERN

In the snapshot of any particular moment a particular participation pattern can be observed in every group. For example, it may be all *one way* traffic, with the leader or some other member conducting a monologue; or it may be *two-way*, with the leader talking to members and members responding to him; or it may be *multidirectional*, with all members talking to one another and to the group as a whole.

In any given group you may notice that one of these patterns tends to be prevalent over a period of time. In other groups there may be a considerable variation within quite short spaces.

There is no reason to believe that any one pattern of participation is always best: it depends upon the situation. But many studies point to the common sense conclusion that the more that members participate the more they will tend to be involved in the group.

It should not be assumed, of course, that a silent member is necessarily uninterested. The member may be simply thinking. As leader, you should ask yourself the following questions about them. Are they really interested? What prevents them from speaking? It may be that they want to speak but never have the opportunity to join in the discussion because someone (is it you?) is talking overmuch. If so, you should practise the skill of *gate-keeping*: 'Malcolm, we have heard your views at some length but Sally hasn't said anything for the last hour, though doubtless she has been thinking a lot. Sally, have you anything to contribute to next year's objectives on the marketing front . . . No, Malcolm you can't just clarify your last point (laughter) – Sally?'

It is very easy, and often useful in teambuilding, to chart the participation pattern during a defined period of discussion, thus providing some objective data about this aspect of group working, as in the diagram below.

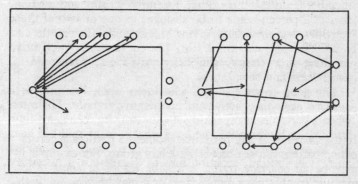

Fig. 2.1   Participation Patterns

CHECKLIST

- How much of the talking is done by the leader, how much is done by the other members?

- To whom are questions usually addressed – the group as a whole, the leader, or particular members?

- Do the members who don't talk much appear to be interested and listening alertly (nonverbal participation), or do they seem bored and apathetic?

- Do the leader and other senior members in the group practise gate-keeping skills – to open the door for lower status members to talk?

COMMUNICATION

How well do group members understand each other's meanings: how clearly are they communicating their ideas, values and feelings? If some members, for instance, are using a highly specialised technical vocabulary they may be talking over the heads of the rest of the group.

Sometimes a group will develop a specialised vocabulary of its own, a kind of verbal shorthand, or private jokes that aren't understood by new members or outsiders. That can facilitate communication within the group, but can create problems within the organisation as a whole.

Communication in a group will be greatly enhanced if each member is skilled in speaking, listening, writing and reading. In fact a person tends to be stronger in one or two of these activities than the others, giving him a profile of strengths and weaknesses as a communicator. The cornerstones of effective speaking are: clarity, simplicity, vividness, preparedness, naturalness and conciseness.

The good listener is one who looks upon listening as a positive, searching, active and cooperative activity. Too often when a person is not speaking at a meeting he spends his time framing his intervention: he *hears* what is being said but does not *listen* in a way that grasps the core meaning of someone else's contribution, enabling him to elucidate it if necessary and build upon it or weave it into the discussion.

Even nonverbal communication can often be eloquent. A person's posture, facial expression and gestures, tell a great deal about what he is thinking and feeling. The member who pulls his chair, for example, away from the table and gazes out of the window is saying something to you and the rest of the group.

CHECKLIST

- Are members expressing their ideas clearly, simply and concisely?

- Are visual aids and other communication aids used in a way that suggests thorough preparation by members?

- Do any general concepts, such as 'maximum profit' or 'customer service' get sufficiently defined so that the group agrees on their meaning?

- Do members often adopt contributions previously made and build their ideas on to them?

- Do members feel free to ask for clarification when they don't understand a statement?

- Are responses to statements frequently irrelevant?

COHESIVENESS

The cohesiveness of a group is determined by the strength of the bonds that bind the individual parts together into a unified whole. This property is related to other more traditional concepts such as morale and team spirit. Cohesiveness, the strength of attraction of the group for its members, is also linked to the degree of interest commitment to the common task. It is sometimes referred to as the 'we-feeling' of a group – the extent to which members talk in terms of 'we' and 'us'. Symptoms of low cohesion include the absence of such words from the group's vocabulary.

Many studies have identified the conditions under which groups will tend to become more cohesive. The more important factors are:

- *Physical proximity*
  People working together in the same place will tend to form a group, even if their work is not interdependent. Length of time together increases the tendency towards cohesiveness.

- *Same or similar work*
  People doing identical or similar work are faced with the same problems and can help each other in various ways – a source of group formation.

- *Homogeneity*
  Cohesiveness in groups tends to be greater if members share such characteristics as race, age, sex, social status and attitudes or values.

- *Personality*
  Members do not have to be alike in personality, but some combinations of personality work better than others – where social needs are strong and there are not too many over-dominant or disruptive people.

- *Communication*
  Cohesiveness will be greater if members can communicate easily with others, and less if distance, noise or organisational arrangements make communication difficult.

- *Size*
  It becomes more difficult for groups of more than 12 or 15 members to develop group cohesion. Small groups are much more likely to do so.

Cohesiveness – the magnetic attraction of members to the invisible centre of the group – is enhanced if belonging to it is *rewarding* to individuals in several ways. Studies have confirmed that members are most likely to be attracted to a group if it has a successful record in competition with other groups. High pay and prestige, the consequences of belonging to such successful groups, are also incentives for wanting to be or remain a member.

Methods of pay or working conditions can foster or retard the development of group cohesiveness in industry. A group bonus scheme rather than individual incentive schemes, for example, emphasises the shared nature of the common task. The efforts of each member of the assembly line or research group will then serve the interests of all the others. But strong group pressures may then build up on slow workers who are holding back the team. Such a 'passenger' may be forced out of the group.

Group cohesiveness is a double-edged weapon. Fig. 2.2 lists the pros and cons of the cohesive group.

Advantages	Disadvantages
Greater co-operation	Life more difficult for new entrants
More/easier communication	Restricts entry for new ideas
Increased resistance to frustration	Resists changes in work practices
Reduced labour turnover	
Lower absenteeism	Seen as awkward/ combative by other groups, thus reducing intergroup co-operation
Low tolerance of 'slackers'	

Fig. 2.2   The Cohesive Group

A leader should always be on the alert for the unwanted side effects of group cohesiveness. Thus, one of a leader's jobs is to protect individuals against the power of the group. Group power can sometimes be exercised unfairly on individuals for a variety of reasons. Groups can make an individual into a scapegoat, for example, as if tacitly agreeing to make him responsible for the whole burden of corporate failure. The psychology of this act, probably largely unconscious, is quite different from the proper doctrine of individual accountability, a dimension which should not be cancelled by group membership.

Any form of such victimisation should be stopped by the leader if for no other reason than that it will eventually destroy the group's unity.

The essentials of morale

'Morale is a state of mind. It is that intangible force which will move a whole group of men to give their last ounce to achieve something, without counting the cost to themselves; that makes them feel they are part of something greater than themselves. If they are to feel that, their morale must, if it is to endure – and the essence of morale is that it should endure – have certain foundations. These foundations are spiritual, intellectual and material, and that is their order of importance. Spiritual first, because only spiritual foundations can stand real strain. Next intellectual, because men are swayed by reason as well as feeling. Material last – important, but last – because the very highest kinds of morale are often met when material conditions are lowest.'

Field Marshal Lord Slim, in
Defeat into Victory (1956)

Group cohesiveness is not the same as morale, although they are like cousins. Morale was a word introduced in the last century to describe a group's or individual's *condition* in relation to confidence, discipline and sense of common purpose. It covers the condition of people's attitudes to the task, their loyalty to one another and their self-respect. The links of morale with *esprit de corps* and group cohesiveness are obvious. When morale is high men carry out work in the face of danger or difficulty. When it is low men are more vulnerable to criticism, hardship and failure.

CHECKLIST

- How well is the group working together as a unit?

- What subgroups or 'lone wolves' are there and how do they affect the group?

- What evidence is there of interest or lack of interest on the part of members of the group (or groups in the organisation) in what is happening in the area of the common task?

- Do members speak to the leader of 'your group' or 'our group'?

- Despite reverses is the level of confidence high? Is there still a strong sense of purpose and resolve?
- Is team spirit in evidence? Do members mutually support and encourage each other as well as working well together in a technical sense?

ATMOSPHERE

Although atmosphere, like morale, is an intangible thing, it is usually fairly easy to sense. It is often referred to as the 'social climate' of the group, with such characteristics as 'warm, friendly, relaxed, informal, free' in contrast to 'cold, hostile, tense, formal, restrained'. Atmosphere affects how members feel about a group and the degree of spontaneity in their participation. Atmosphere may be temporary; climate implies a prevailing condition.

> 'Teams generate a climate of loyalty', writes Tom Douglas, 'which stems from the acceptance of dependence on others to achieve a desired outcome. There is something of the secret society about all successful teams. Members accept the skills and knowledge of other members as a common resource and the sense of sharing and shared experience, which distinguishes members from non-members, is high'.[4]

Atmosphere or climate relates to morale, which is an atmospheric word if ever there was one.

What is the difference between atmosphere and morale? Atmosphere is usually fairly easy to sense: you feel it yourself. On the other hand morale is inferred from observations of behaviour, and it is an inference about the state of people observed. It is a vital part of leadership to build up the right atmosphere or climate and to change if it is wrong. Let me quote some sentences from Montgomery's speech to his staff when he took over the Eighth Army before the Battle of El Alamein:

> You do not know me, I do not know you, but we have got to work together. Therefore, we must understand each other, we must have confidence in each other. I have only been here a few hours, but from what I have seen and heard since I arrived, I am prepared to say here and now that I have confidence in you. We will work together as a team. I believe that one of the

first duties is to create what I call atmosphere. I do not like the general atmosphere I find here – it is an atmosphere of doubt, of looking back. All that must cease. I want to impress upon everyone that the bad times are over and it will be done. If anybody here thinks it cannot be done, let him go at once. I do not want any doubters. It can be done and it will be done beyond any possibility of doubt.[5]

Morale

Morale
Shows itself
As a state of mind
Radiating confidence
In people

Where each member
Feels sure of his own niche,
Stands on his own abilities
And works out his own solutions
– Knowing he is
Part of a team

Where no person
Feels anxiety or fear
Or pressure to be better
Than someone else

Where there exists
A sharing of ideas
A freedom to plan
A sureness of worth,
And a knowledge
That help is available
For the asking

To the end that
People grow and mature
Warmed by a friendly climate

Anon

The above verses, it should be noted, describes some valuable inward features of a work group, but it does not touch the way in which it responds to outer events. The latter is also a vital dimension of morale.

Mark Twain once said: 'Everyone talks about the weather but no one does anything about it'. You can affect the climate in your organisation by what you are, what you do, and what you say.

CHECKLIST

- Would you describe your primary work group as warm or cool, friendly or hostile, relaxed or tense, informal or formal, free or restrained?

- Can opposing views or negative feelings be expressed without fear of retribution?

- Is morale in the group low? Is there an 'atmosphere of doubt, of looking back'?

STANDARDS

Every group, if it is together for some time, develops a code of conduct or set of standards about what is proper and acceptable behaviour. These include such subjects as what matters may be discussed, what is taboo (such as religion or politics); how well members listen to each other's opinions; how far it is proper to volunteer one's services; the length and intensity of work that's considered right and fair; whether or not pilfering is permissible, and many more 'do's and don'ts'.

It may be difficult for a new member to identify and adopt a group's standards if they differ from those of other groups he has experienced, for these standards are usually implicit rather than written down. Indeed, at a given time, a group might be confused about what its own standards actually are.

A group-norm – an oft-used phrase in the textbooks – is simply an authoritative standard. Norm derives from the Latin word for a builder's or carpenter's square, the tool which gives him the perfect right angle.

Over-conformity to accepted norms can stultify growth and inhibit creativity. For creative individuals will always tend to deviate from or transcend the established ways of doing things or thinking about the world in which the group is set. Therefore norms can be battle lines between groups and individuals. This tension is the theme of a later chapter.

Standards can be broken down into different families, which to some extent function differently:

- **Work**   These concern the best and easiest methods of working, and usually include some unwritten folklore: how fast, how hard, how long, to what standard, how safety-minded and so on. Professional training seeks to inculcate certain standards of conduct so that individuals follow them whatever the social pressures or when they are working on their own.

- **Attitudes**   Attitudes, beliefs and values tend to be shared in groups. The fact that a group accepts a common attitude does not of course mean it is necessarily true. Groups may also share a common interpretation of the past, often coloured by some collective myths!

- *Interpersonal behaviour*

There are norms about what can be discussed and what cannot, whether or not it is right to interrupt, where to go for lunch and so on. Such tacit agreements to proceed socially in a standard way helps to make the behaviour of others predictable, orderly and satisfying. Shared routines can be enjoyed. Norms keep interpersonal conflicts to the minimum; they avoid conflicts over such potential problems as helping, allocation of jobs and division of rewards.

- *Clothes and language*

Members of a group usually resemble each other in their dress and physical appearance for example, haircut. They often use a private language of their own: slang, technical terms related to the job, nicknames for people and places, sub-cultural vocabularies, such as obscenities. Especially prevalent in what have vividly been called 'ball and chain groups'.

- *Moral standards*

These range from the permissible limits of time-wasting, scrounging, cheating on incentive schemes to norms concerning ethical practice, truth-telling and sexual behaviour.

Standards begin life as a rough-and-ready form of consensus among the original members of the group as to what will work for them if they are to attain their goals and hold together in unity. Some members – the leader or leading members – have more influence over this process than others. These latter, less influential members, together with all new recruits to the group, are expected to adopt these norms. Several factors are at work to help them to do so.

In the first instance people falling short of a norm or consciously choosing to deviate from it become the target for a great deal of persuasion and friendly pressure to conform from the majority. They can conform or leave the group. If they continue to stand out they risk punishment. There is a Japanese proverb, much quoted today in Japan, which says that the nail that sticks up is going to get knocked on the head.

The mildest form of punishment is group displeasure. As that escalates the treatment of deviants becomes more severe. When in difficulties they receive no help; they are given the worst jobs; their work is interfered with. They may be rejected, given the silent treatment or 'sent to Coventry' in the English phrase, or even physically attacked. It is as if the group has reserves of the milk of human kindness; once these have been exhausted it can turn nasty.

It is impossible to avoid the moral issue here. First you have to decide if the norm being urged is good or bad. Then you have to decide whether or not the form of group pressure being applied is justifiable or not in the circumstances.

In normal situations we do not have to make these judgements solely on our own or from scratch. Society has a tradition of social and moral norms, the minimum standards among them being enshrined in constitutions and laws. The *law* does also rule out many of the obvious abuses of group power over deviant individuals. You can reason with a strike-breaking colleague; you cannot – or rather should not – break his arm.

CHECKLIST

- Can you identify any unwritten standards in the group?

- Are there marked deviations from these standards by one or more members?

- Do these standards seem to be well understood by all members, or is there confusion about them?

- Which of the group's standards seem to help, and which seem to hinder the group's progress?

STRUCTURE AND ORGANISATION

Groups have both a formal and an informal organisational structure. The formal structure, which might be highly visible (officers, committees, appointed positions) represents the division of labour among members so that essential functions are performed. Beyond formal structure there is also informal, much of which comes into play behind the scenes. It concerns how things actually get done according to the relative prestige, influence, power, seniority and persuasiveness of members.

The concept of roles, discussed in the next chapter, is related to structure. Structure can almost be defined as a *hierarchy* of roles within the group or organisation.

Structure in work groups ought to be directly related to the common task. In so far as the needs of the task are changing, so structure should be flexible or malleable to alteration. Ideally there should not be a dichotomy or chasm between the formal and informal structures. Although all organisations should encourage communication outside 'proper channels', the better designed they are the less chance should there be that they are run on some secret 'old boy net'.

CHECKLIST

- What kind of formal structure or organisation is there within the group?
- What is the invisible structure: who really controls; who defers to others?
- Is the structure understood and accepted by the members?
- Is it appropriate to the group's purpose and tasks?

GROUPS IN MOTION

So far we have been looking at some of the key elements or variables that make up a group – its properties or dimensions – from an analytical point of view, rather as if we are dissecting a dead fish. But groups are alive; they do not stand still in time and space. The analytical approach needs to be complemented by a holistic view of the moving, living, dynamic whole. Until you have seen a shoal of fish gliding together, suddenly turning silver-sided around an invisible centre of gravity, you have not understood groups.

Not only is the group moving as a unit, but the various elements within it are constantly interacting. A change in procedure will affect the atmosphere, which will affect the participation pattern, which will affect cohesion, which will affect morale and so on.

Various attempts have been made to discern phases or patterns within the constant flux of group life.

Many theorists in the Group Dynamics movement, for example, made analogies describing the process of group formation as a spiral, a series of cycles, or a series of stages which succeed each other as growth occurs.

Groups would work on a problem, and then as if by agreement withdraw from it, only to return to the same ground some time later but upon a higher plane. Knowledge of this spiralling effect was useful not least because it helped me as a teacher to time my interventions. For instance, it was worth waiting for the 'upward thermals' before making comments. Remarks made when the group was not in a work phase or cycle, but 'resting' or withdrawing, were not as likely to be effective.

Consistent and identifiable stages of development in all groups probably do not exist. Group growth is a gradual process in which themes and subtleness may intertwine but in which the dramatic quality is the wholeness. The closest analogy to my mind is a musical symphony, with tunes, phrases, moods interwoven into a moving pattern.

Any breakdown into phases by a process of analysis therefore runs the double danger of over-simplifying and also destroying that very holistic quality which constitutes the group. Analysis leads to abstraction, which in turn leads us away from the concrete, unique, whole group with whom you may be working the design office or its equivalent.

There are probably no clear and finite *stages* of development. But that does not mean there are no consistent sequential changes. Not every teenager goes through a stage of moodiness, but there are changes in that period of life which tend to be accompanied by moodiness. Not every mother feels postnatal depression, but there is a strong tendency for that to happen.

This is the nearest we can get to regularity. It does appear that in some groups change takes a cyclic or spiral form, with movement backwards and forwards. In other groups change seems to happen in sudden leaps and bounds, interspersed with plateau periods where no change occurs. In other groups there are regressive movements as well as dramatic and unpredictable spurts. Again you may be able to think of analogies in the development of individuals you know well – or indeed in your own life history. You should bear these factors in mind when considering the group development model in Fig. 2.3.

	Group structure	Task activity
Forming	Considerable anxiety, testing to discover the nature of the situation, what help can be expected from leader or convener and what behaviour will or will not be appropriate.	What is the task? Members seek the answers to that basic question, together with knowledge of the rules and the methods to be employed.
Storming	Conflict emerges between sub-groups; the authority and/or competence of the leader is challenged. Opinions polarise. Individuals react against efforts of the leader or group to control them.	The value and feasibility of the task is questioned. People react emotionally against its demands.
Norming	The group begins to harmonise; it experiences group cohesion or unity for the first time. Norms emerge as those in conflict are reconciled and resistance is overcome. Mutual support develops.	Co-operation on the task begins; plans are made and work standards laid down. Communication of views and feelings develop.
Performing	The group structures itself or accepts a structure which fits most appropriately its common task. Roles are seen in terms functional to the task and flexibility between them develops.	Constructive work on the task surges ahead; progress is experienced as more of the group's energy is applied to being effective in the area of their common task.

Fig. 2.3 Group Development

These phrases are fairly recognisable to any normally perceptive person with experience in work groups. Where there is an unresolved problem of who is in charge, for example, a power struggle may develop among members who desire to have things move their way or who may enjoy controlling others or power for its own sake. Such people in such unresolved control situations will tend to engage in various persuasive methods of controlling others, such as advice giving, argument or confrontation. Strategies for manipulating others may be resorted to, possibly in sub-groups outside the total group. People may appeal in vain to the appointed or elected leader to check this competition for power. Others may argue against all forms of control, as if enjoying the apparent freedom in lack of any organisation.

The resolution of this phase, and the eventual emergence of the group into the stage of *performance*, is not the end of the story. The group which is already a team in ore may go on to become the refined metal of a high performance team. The processes by which high tempered steel can be refined and wrought from the dull ore of average performance are the theme of Part Two.

The group may equally lapse into decline, the *dorming* phase. Here, group structure becomes governed by routine and systems – everything has to go through 'proper channels' and the group spirit becomes ossified into a comfortable and cosy togetherness. Task activity falls off in quantity and quality, but the group does not really mind . . . it is so tired . . . yawn, yawn. It is so satisfied by past achievements that it is content to leave the unconquered peaks to the young thrusting groups coming into being all around them.

Not all groups behave in this way. Some complete their job and disperse. Some complete a job and say 'that was enjoyable – can we find something else to do.'

POINTS TO PONDER

Groups share a number of properties which can to some extent be abstracted and discussed in general. They include a common background or history (or lack of it), participation patterns, communication, cohesiveness, atmosphere, standards, structure and organisation.

Groups change and grow because they exist in time as well

as space. Seek to understand the processes at work within them as they move forwards by fits and starts, progressing and regressing. Then you will be in a better position to intervene helpfully.

Four simple stages – forming, storming, norming and performing – will serve you as a good introduction to the story, especially if you are present at the birth of a new group.

Group cohesiveness is essential – but remember that it brings some potential disadvantages in its train. As a leader you must always watch out for these danger signs and then take action to counter them.

Watch out, too, for the group norms. Are they as you would want them to be? If not, change them by your words and examples.

To lead is to serve, nothing more and nothing less.

3 Roles

A role is a capacity in which someone acts in relation to others. It is a metaphor from the theatre, where a role is a part assumed by one actor in a play while others are assuming other parts.

This origin gives the word some persistent undertones. A dramatic role is acted or played; it is taken on temporarily and dropped at the end of the play.

But having a role in real life need not connote 'play-acting' or temporariness. Rightly understood, the concept can illuminate behaviour in work groups, families and society.

VARIETIES OF ROLE

Role tends to be a favourite word among sociologists. But in my opinion to apply it to all social relations, however transitory or spontaneous, is to water down the concept to the point where it becomes vacuous and useless.

A role in the untheatrical sense, in the context of work groups and families, organisations and communities, should usually be reserved for those relationships which are sufficiently structured to have a common name, such as teacher-pupil, leader-follower, doctor-patient, husband-wife. Role behaviour is the way of acting which is considered appropriate to a role. Various factors – functional, traditional or custom – shape what is thought to be this appropriate behaviour.

An important insight from social studies is that the 'occupant' of a role is to some degree the recipient of *expectations* from others as to what behaviour is appropriate to his role. If a policeman stops your car in heavy traffic in order to tell you a joke you may be justifiably apprehensive: he has stepped outside his role. You do not *expect* him to behave like that.

The concept of role, then, can be applied to life. Indeed the Greeks had a proverb: 'Life is a stage, so learn to play your part'. Shakespeare's words echo that thought:

> All the world's a stage,
> And all the men and women merely players:
> They have their exits and their entrances;
> And one man in his time plays many parts,
> His acts being seven ages. At first the infant,
> Mewling and puking in the nurse's arms.
> And then . . .

In these oft-quoted lines from *As You Like It* Shakespeare goes on to list the seven ages of a man's life, characterising three of them by the roles in a contemporary drama which the youth and mature man might play during these seven ages: lover, soldier and magistrate.

Real life is inevitably more complex, but the rough division of roles between family life and work in Shakespeare's list is perpetuated on this wider front. Our roles, of course, change suddenly or subtly as we move through Shakespeare's seven ages of man. Here are some examples:

Family roles	*Work roles*
son or daughter	foreman
husband or wife	supervisor
father or mother	shop steward
grandfather or mother	manager
aunt or uncle	managing director
brother or sister	senior trades union official
and so on	chairman

We can distinguish between the more *formal* roles, such as being a judge, and the more *informal* ones, such as lover and friend. The latter are found more in the sphere of personal relationships. In working groups, you should note here that the role of leader is sometimes formal (for example, the appointed Squadron Leader of a fighter squadron) and sometimes more informal, the leader who emerges naturally from the group and has no official position.

Roles are also connected with *status* or social position in work groups and organisations. As we have seen, as part of group structuring, different individuals will occupy different roles. Low status members at meetings will be recognisable because they will not talk much, be polite, deferential and generally have little notice taken of them.

Thus some form of *hierarchy* or 'pecking order' emerges in all groups. Financial reward, rank and status often go together but not by any means always. Sometimes status (as in the British honours system) is divorced from financial reward.

In working groups the role that naturally carries the highest status is that of the leader. He or she heads the hierarchy, implicit or explicit, within the group. To this key role we must now turn.

THE ROLE OF LEADER

It is now widely accepted that the most important role in a small work group is that of the leader. We should attempt to distinguish here, as always, between the *role* and the *person* performing the role. A role can be seen in general and impersonal terms. We can shape our notion of a role by looking objectively at the situation, at the rights and obligations involved, and above all at the requirements of the task to be done. Some roles, however, are likely to call for certain personal qualities. Leadership is clearly in this category. Every individual leader who fulfils the leadership role will therefore do so in his own unique style, governed by the unique combination of traits – personality and character – he brings to the role.

Despite these personal differences I have argued that the core role of all leaders is the same. The role is to help the group to achieve its common task, to maintain it as a unity and to ensure that each individual contributes his best.

That definition, to repeat the point, applies to leaders in all working situations, at any level of structure in their role relationships, whether they are formal or informal, elected or appointed, imposed or emergent.

This view of leadership role differed from that taught in the Group Dynamics movement. There the leadership role as such was certainly not emphasised. 'Most groups do have appointed leaders', conceded Matthew B. Miles, an influential figure in the movement, 'as a kind of 'safety net' or guarantee that *someone* will fill needed functions, but the approach taken here assumes that the appointed leader and members alike may exert leadership'.[6]

This underestimate of the role of leadership in the Group Dynamics movement, noted critically by early commentators[7] and repaired later in the work of some social psychologists,[8] stemmed from the unique situational factors I have already mentioned.

ROLE CONFLICT

Role conflict exists at work as well. Whatever the job titles, managers occupy three roles. The first – leader – is so pre-occupying that the other two – the roles of follower or *subordinate* and *colleague* – are often overlooked. The latter two roles are more shadowy. But there can be considerable tensions between your obligations to the group working for you and your loyalty to your superior or your co-operation with colleagues of the same status as yourself in other parts of the organisation. Each man is a trinity of three persons.

Role conflict in that sense does not exhaust the stress problems related to work roles, as the following chart illustrates.

Lack of clarity and comfort in your role can cause insecurity, lack of confidence, irritation, anxiety and even anger among those around you. All these add up to unwelcome stress. As we all know, a challenge can be invigorating. But it can easily degenerate into a form of stress which is by definition damaging. There is a world of difference between working under pressure and working under strain. The symptoms of such *role strain* are:

- *Stress*   Often accompanied by physical symptoms.
                           Behaviour characterised by: irritability,
                           scrupulous concern for trivial detail;
                           emphasis on precision; a tendency to
                           dichotomise things into 'black' or 'white';
                           resort to stereotyped responses; increased
                           sensitivity to group pressures and
                           organisational rumours.

- *Low Morale*   Often expressed as: dissatisfaction with the
                           job; cynical comments about the
                           organisation; low confidence in colleagues
                           and subordinates; a sense of futility.

- *Communication*   Often the person becomes preoccupied, silent
  difficulties   and withdrawn. He is hard to talk to.

These symptoms, of course, may be associated with stress
arising from sources other than role strain. If the underlying
problem is to do with roles, then action should be taken as
suggested in Fig. 3.1.

Problem	Causes	Strategies
Role conflict	Results from the necessity for a person to carry out two or more roles in the same situation where the expectations connected with each role are in conflict.	Reduce the importance of one of the roles. Agree a compartmentalisation of one's life, for example, weekends for families.
Role incompatibility	This arises when there are rival expectations about the same role. For instance, your supervisor may expect you to manage in a certain way while your subordinates may have totally different expectations.	Decide to give priority to the expectations of the more important people, down-grading the expectations of the others. Ask for a resolution of the incompatibility from them.

Problem	Causes	Strategies
Role overload	Not the same as work overload. It comes when a person has too many roles for him to handle at a time. It is the variety rather than the quantity of work which is experienced here as confusing and tiring.	Down-grade the priority level of some roles, accepting from self a lower performance level. Agree a re-assignment of role responsibilities.
Role underload	This occurs characteristically when an individual is given a role which falls far short of his self-concept. Whether it is or not is irrelevant: it is the individual's perception which causes role underload.	Take on someone else's role in addition to your own. Use your imagination to develop the role.
Role ambiguity	Arises when there is uncertainty in the mind of the focal person or members of his group, colleagues or superiors as to precisely what his role is at any given time. Ambiguity is not necessarily a bad thing; it can aid creativity. But uncertainty can be experienced as unhelpful and stressful.	Ask for clarification from key members of the organisation with a stake in the problem. Negotiate with them a clearer concept of your role.

Fig. 3.1   Role Problems

POINTS TO PONDER

Just as we buy our clothes ready-made 'off the peg' so most of the roles we occupy or aspire to at work exist in their own right. A team can be thought of as a structure of jobs.

If a relationship moves into action then roles will begin to emerge. Conversely, if you start with a role, it will tell you what actions and relationships are expected from you.

Roles should never be completely defined even if that was possible – that would leave no room for your creativity as a person. But you should strive to be as clear as possible about any given role.

Many people have impoverished concepts of the roles they occupy. Draw upon as many sources as you can to enlarge and deepen your understanding of these roles.

This applies especially to the three basic roles at work – *leader, subordinate* and *colleague*.

Role without personality is empty, but personality without role is ineffective

4 Member functions

Perhaps the most enduring contribution of the study of group dynamics to our understanding of groups is the distinction between *task* and *maintenance* behaviour. Task behaviour is self-explanatory. In this context maintenance means holding the group together or maintaining it as a unity.

This discovery of two distinct areas of concern and response in groups was a real milestone. The ways in which people responded could be categorised in terms of *functions* – what you *do* or *say* rather than what you *are* as a person. Much previous talk about functions in organisations could now be earthed in the empirically-discovered realities of group life: *the need to achieve the common task and the need to be held together as a working entity.*

There was another important distinction concerning group work made in Group Dynamics: this time *content* and *process*. The content is what the group is talking about, while process concerns such issues as how it makes decisions. Everyone knows what a process is, but it is still very difficult to define it. The application of heat to uncooked food is the 'process' of cooking: it changes materials from one form to another.

There is a potential confusion here, because the contrast cannot be equated with that between task and maintenance. They are different sets of ideas.

TASK AND GROUP MAINTÈNANCE FUNCTIONS

In Chapter 2 we looked at what happens in the early life of a group. It must be reiterated that the groups which formed the subject of these studies were training groups in the Group Dynamics movement, and that consequently they were rather peculiar if not unique.

The impact of situational influences was not so readily understood then as now. Therefore hesitation is called for before transferring lessons to work group settings which may be familiar to you in real life. Nevertheless, I hold that the Group Dynamics movement did throw up some valuable insights relevant to all who work with groups, insights which we would be foolish to let slip into obscurity.

It is especially important to bear this provenance in mind when reading the next few pages on functions. They are based on the work of Kenneth D. Benne and Paul Sheats in 1948[9]. Their lists of functions clearly relate to the unstructured discussion group-type situation. Indeed Benne and Sheats developed their lists of functions for the First National Training Laboratory in Group Development, held in America in 1947. The lists followed closely the analysis of participation functions as used in coding the content and process of group discussions for their research purposes.

You will notice that the authors talk about member *roles* rather than *functions*. To personalise functions like that strikes me as wrong, a point I shall return to later. For my part I prefer to keep the word role for relationships with some more marked degree of structure, ones with a pattern of conduct associated with them – recognised in breach as well as in observance. I should emphasise again that if any form of social relation, however transitory or spontaneous, came to be regarded as a role relation, the concept will become so general and all-embracing as to lose its value as a tool of social analysis. However, I have felt it right here to reproduce the categories exactly in the way that Benne and Sheats wrote them.

GROUP TASK ROLES

Benne and Sheats assumed that they were dealing with a discussion group and that its task was roughly to select, define and solve common problems. The roles they identified relate to functions of facilitating and co-ordinating these group problem-solving activities. The inappropriateness of their use of the word 'role' is underlined when they go on to say that 'each member may of course enact more than one role in any given unit of participation and a wide range of roles in successive participations'. Here are their twelve categories:

Initiator-contributor Suggests to group new ideas, new group goals, or new definition of problem; proposes new procedures, ways of handling some difficulty or forms of organisation.

Information seeker Asks for clarification of suggestions in terms of factual accuracy; seeks information and facts relevant to problem.

Opinion seeker Asks not for facts but for clarification of the values pertinent to what the group is undertaking or involved in the various suggestions.

Information giver Offers facts or generalisations which are 'authoritative' or relates his own experience to the group problem.

Opinion giver States his belief or opinion pertinently to a suggestion made or alternatives being canvassed.

Elaborator Spells out suggestions in terms of examples or developed meanings; offers reasons for suggestions and tries to deduce consequences of following them.

Co-ordinator Shows or clarifies the relationships among various ideas and suggestions and tries to pull them together; attempts to co-ordinate the activities of members or sub-group.

Orienter	Defines the position of the group with respect to its goals; summarises what has happened; points to departures from agreed directions; raises questions upon direction which the group discussion is taking.
Evaluator-critic	Subjects the accomplishment of the group to some standard or set of standards.
Energiser	Prods the group to action or decision; attempts to stimulate or arouse the group to 'greater' or 'higher quality' activity.
Procedural technician	Expedites group movement by doing things for the group, performing routine tasks, for example distributing materials, rearranging seats, operating tape-recorder.
Recorder	Writes down suggestions, makes a record of group decisions; acts as 'group memory'.

GROUP BUILDING AND MAINTENANCE ROLES

Here the analysis of member functions focuses on those contributions which have for their purpose, according to Benne and Sheats, 'the building of group-centred attitudes and orientation among the members of a group or the maintenance and perpetuation of such group-centred behaviour. A given contribution may involve several roles, and a member or the 'leader' may perform various roles in successive contributions. Here they offered seven categories:

Encourager	Praises, agrees with and accepts the contribution of others; indicates warmth and solidarity in his attitude toward other group members; indicates understanding and acceptance of other points of view, ideas and suggestions.
Harmoniser	Mediates the differences between other members; attempts to reconcile disagreements, relieves tension in conflict situations through humour, pouring oil on troubled waters, and so on.

Compromiser	Operates from within a conflict in which his idea or position is involved. He may offer compromise by yielding status, admitting his error, by disciplining himself to maintain group harmony or by 'coming half-way' in moving along with the group.
Gatekeeper-expediter	Attempts to keep communication channels open by encouraging or facilitating the participation of others ('we haven't heard the ideas of Mr X yet', and so on); proposes regulating flow of information, for example limits on length of contributions so all can have a say.
Standard setter	Expresses standards for the group or applies standards in evaluating the quality of group process.
Group observer-commentator	Keeps records of various aspects of group process and feeds such data with proposed interpretations into the group's evaluation of its own procedures.
Follower	Goes along with the movement of the group, more or less passively accepting the ideas of others, serving as audience in group discussion and decision.

INDIVIDUAL ROLES

Benne and Sheats included a section on 'individual' roles (their quotes). They obviously viewed these behaviours unfavourably. Attempts by 'members of a group to satisfy individual needs which are irrelevant to the group task and which are non-oriented or negatively oriented to group building and maintenance set problems of group and member training. A high incidence of "individual-centred" as opposed to "group-centred" participation in a group always calls for self-diagnosis of the group'.

They identified eight such 'unhelpful' individual roles:

Aggressor	Deflates status of others; expresses disapproval of the values, acts or feelings of others; attacks group or the problem it is working on; jokes aggressively; shows envy towards others.
Blocker	Tends to be negative and stubbornly resistant; disagrees and opposes without or beyond reason; attempts to maintain or bring back an issue after the group has rejected or by-passed it.
Recognition-seeker	Works in various ways to call attention to himself: boasting, reporting on personal achievements, acting in unusual ways or struggling to prevent his being placed in an 'inferior' position.
Self-confessor	Uses the audience opportunity which the group setting provides to express personal, non-group oriented ideas, feelings and insights.
Playboy	Makes a display of his lack of involvement in the group's processes, in the form of cynicism, nonchalance, horseplay and other less studied forms of 'out of school' behaviour.
Dominator	Tries to assert authority or superiority in manipulating the group or certain members of the group, by for example flattery, asserting superior status or right to attention, giving directions authoritatively, interrupting the contributions of others.
Help-seeker	Attempts to call forth 'sympathy' response from other members or the whole group, through expressions of insecurity, personal confusion or depreciation of himself beyond reason.
Special interest pleader	Speaks for the 'small businessman', the 'grass roots' community, the 'housewife', all 'work people' and so on, usually cloaking his own prejudices or biases in the stereotype which best fits his individual need.

FUNCTIONS IN PERSPECTIVE

The notes on these roles give you a fair idea of the kind of behaviour which you might have observed if you had been sitting in on one of the American T-groups in the 1950s and 1960s. Observation of task, group and individual behaviour using the Benne-Sheats forms played a prime part in sensitivity training – sensitivity to the variety of roles and sensitivity to the roles one played oneself and their effects on others.

You can see that although the three headings of *Task*, *Group* and *Individual* are already present in embryo, the functions (alias roles) described are very dependent upon the unstructured and so-called 'leaderless' created group setting. In Chapter 6 these functions are developed to accord more with real life situations.

You will have noticed the rather ambivalent overtones concerning the individual in the Group Dynamics movement. Unless he is subordinating himself to the group in some way the individual is seen as rather a nuisance. This anti-individualism of Group Dynamics later attracted much criticism from writers such as William H. Whyte, author of the influential book *The Organisational Man* (1955).[10] Psychologists who became prominent prophets in the 1960s – notably A.H. Maslow and Fred Herzberg – joined in the attack. In the next chapter I shall present my own philosophy of groups and persons within them.

When you read the description of 'individual roles' by Benne and Sheats – essentially seen as irrelevant to the group – you can see why the American schools of social psychology concentrated exclusively on the *task* and *group maintenance* (alias human relations or socio-emotional behaviour) areas, and virtually dropped the third area – the *individual* – completely. American theorists, such as Blake and Mouton, Hersey and Blanchard, worked with this restricted palette of the *two* dimensions of task and human relations, whereas in the United Kingdom I continued to develop the *three* circles as a whole. In the next chapter the third dimension – the individual – will be explored in a much more positive way.

POINTS TO PONDER

Group life can be analysed in several ways. There is the distinction between *content* and *process*. Content is what is being discussed, while process is *how* the group is functioning. Another related but different distinction was between behaviour related to the *task* and behaviour related to the *maintenance* of the group, and that which merely expressed *individual* idiosyncrasies.

These pioneer studies, in many respects unsatisfactory from the viewpoint of today, form the starting point for our modern functional understanding of leadership.

You should practise observation in small groups. The categories listed in this chapter can be used for this purpose – providing you do not take them too seriously. Aim to become a participant-observer.

Effective groups develop when each member is contributing to the common task and to building the group

5 The individual

Groups are, first of all, collections of individuals. An understanding of groups, therefore, has to start with an understanding of individuals. But how do you do that? It could be argued that it is impossible to understand individuals *in general* – for that is a contradiction in terms. If you want to know Bill you must talk to him, study him and read his life story. No amount of reading books about men in general will help you. Bill is Bill.

Although that argument is partly true it is also partly false. For, in its extreme form, it assumes that Bill is *totally* unique. But in fact, different as Bill is, he shares certain factors or elements which are common to all other individuals. What are they?

Here then is the beginnings of a strategy for getting to know individuals. We need: (1) to understand what is common to all of us, what it can be predicted that all individuals will be or do; and (2) to grasp also what is different, special or in our experience unique about this particular person. The art is to maintain a balance between these two perspectives.

In this chapter I shall present my own philosophy of the person in the group, the relation of group or social life to being an individual.

WHAT IS COMMON TO ALL INDIVIDUALS?

Humans, as we all know, have much in common with animals: the needs for food and shelter, security and self-preservation, for instance. For that matter we share some of the characteristics of machines: input of raw materials, conversion to energy and outputs. These two models – animals and machines – do not, however, take us very far into the territory of human nature.

Our social nature has its roots in our evolutionary past and to some extent we share that too with animals. Various species of animals, birds, fish or insects vary in the extent to which they are social. Some creatures live and hunt alone, except for the mating activity. Our nearest relations – gorillas, apes and chimpanzees – are clearly nearer to the social end of the spectrum.

Yet when we compare our social behaviour to those of apes there are some marked differences as well as similarities. One observation has especially interested me in this context. Before a child is six months old its mother gives it things to clutch in its tiny hands. Gradually the child begins to play a greater part in this game of exchanging for the sake of exchange. By the year's end the baby is making half of the offerings. Baby gorillas don't do it!

In other words, human mothers naturally evoke their child's distinctive human capacity to give and receive. This reciprocity between persons, signified by the giving and receiving of gifts, takes us a long way forwards. Even before a child has anything of its own to give, its parents give it money or things so that it may buy or make presents to give back to them. It is a game that equips the child for full membership in the human family. The essence of that family life is giving and receiving.

In this social context being a *person* – personality – develops. We are persons before being a *particular* person – alias an individual.

It is impossible to think of a person without this social intercourse of giving and receiving. The exchange of gifts, of

course, is symbolic of a deeper willingness to give and receive
in society. We come later to give according to our talents and
abilities; just as we come to receive according to the abilities of
others. We give what we are – just as we may perhaps tend to
become what we give.

There is, I submit, a tendency in human nature, strength-
ened in some children by maladroit parents, to want to take
rather than give, or to take more than we give – taking and
receiving not being quite the same. This inclination or pro-
clivity is a manifestation of a deeper selfishness that can grip
us. Of course, there is a sense in which we have to be selfish or
self-centred in order to survive: it is natural to put oneself
first, although this is balanced in nature by the 'herd instinct',
the desire for the survival of the group or species. But the bias
in human nature towards self, which we can see and resent
without being able to do much about it, can make us grasping,
greedy and covetous in our relationships with others.

There is a conflict between this aspect of human nature not
only with the 'herd instinct' factor for corporate rather than
individual welfare, but also with a natural *moral* law which we
perceive, often in a hazy, distorted or fragmented way, in all
human relationships. This is the law that giving and receiving
should be somehow roughly *equivalent* or equal in value.

There is a special application of this principle of *justice* in
criminal matters, summed up in the proverbial phrase: 'An
eye for an eye, a tooth for a tooth'. The same principle applies
in bartering. Here it is felt that goods traded should be equal
in value. With the introduction of money, primarily as a more
convenient means of exchange, goods or services bought or
sold were supposed to be equal in value to the gold, silver or
copper exchanged for them.

Most social psychologists hold the idea that there is some
form of psychological contact between an individual and a
group, that the rewards of membership will roughly equal the
investment (of time, talents and so on) the individual makes.
Satisfaction is a concept impossible to define precisely, but if
satisfaction as felt by the individual falls below a certain level
he or she will leave the group.

George Homans,[11] for example, suggested that in work
groups people compare their investments and rewards with
those of other people and expect the resulting equation to
reach equal proportions, thus:

$$\frac{\text{My investments}}{\text{His investments}} = \frac{\text{My rewards}}{\text{His rewards}}$$

This equality he calls *distributive justice*. If for various reasons it is out of balance people may feel guilty for having a better investment-reward ratio or resentful at having a worse one than their colleagues. Some studies suggest that failure to maintain distributive justice – perceived unfairness on part of the leader – produces dissatisfaction and declining productivity.

The concept of justice does not exhaust morality; it is only the foundation for human relationships. Being a person leads us to consider the human spirit.

The human spirit is clearly not to be thought of as just one part of our constitution as human beings. Rather it is a way of speaking about that which makes us most truly and fully personal.

The concept of spirit, I suggest, includes the capacity for what could be called self-transcendence. The phrase human spirit is something to do with our extraordinary capacity to reach beyond our limitations, stemming from our consciousness of ourselves as finite, limited individuals. We can, as it were, stand back from ourselves and be aware of ourselves as persons.

One of the deep attractions of teamwork is precisely that membership of a good team does allow us to transcend our own individual limitations of knowledge, ability and performance.

'The joy of working harmoniously with small groups of people who are dedicated to something bigger than themselves, and are completely loyal to each other, counts in my experience as one of the most rewarding things in life', a senior manager told me. Most of us would agree with him.

That is the first step to transcending self-interest. For this capacity for self-transcendence is to be found mainly in our relations with other people. Your spirit, it has been said, is never as uniquely yours as your body, your life or your individuality. It lives only in relation to some other.

Go back for a moment to that moral balance between giving and receiving. When you love someone there may well be occasions when you transcend the rules. You give where there is no hope of return. The coin in which you are paid is joy, which is not the same as pleasure or gratification, but provides a deeper and longer-lasting satisfaction.

In human relations, then, we operate with some notion of justice, in a 'contract' based upon reciprocal and equivalent obligations or responsibilities. But, being persons, we can rise to the call and transcend that contract. Then there is a fuller expression of the human spirit. I love to contemplate that truth: it is so full of hope for the human race.

The concept of being a person in this sense gives us a human right to insist upon being treated as a person – not as an animal, a machine or a thing. We each have an inalienable *dignity* in this sense. We owe it to all persons to require that dignity in us to be at least tacitly accepted or recognised, just as we have to fight if the person in others is being defaced.

Again this constitutes a central moral principle. Take, for example, the relations between the sexes. The fundamental contract is not 'You treat me as a woman, and I'll treat you as a man', though that in some circumstances is a step forward. Nor can the moral contract be rephrased as: 'You treat me as a person, and I'll treat you as a person'. For a moral person there is no such conditional clause. I *must* treat you as a person, whether you respond in kind or not, because you *are* a person. Therefore treating you as a thing – manipulating or using you in any way – will never work, at least in the long run.

These principles about all persons, rather than particular persons, strike me as important in the context of effective teambuilding and leadership for this reason. Your *attitudes* stem ultimately from what beliefs, perceptions or assumptions you hold about human nature. If you get your fundamental picture of man and woman wrong then a degree of falsity will eventually colour your derived attitudes to people at work. You may wish to challenge the view I have expressed here. But I hope that at least my words will have stimulated you to think out your own concept of human nature, so that you are clearer about your values. For if your vision of man is flawed or inadequate, you can be sure that people will become aware of it. Then no accumulation of 'interpersonal skills' or 'behavioural techniques' will save the day for you.

DEVELOPING AS PERSONS

Your characteristics as a person are not wholly determined by the action of the environment; they are also shaped by who you are within yourself as a unique person. Your inheritance provides you with a given nature and potential. The dialogue between you and the world is also to be understood as a dialogue between heredity and environment. In personal terms some of the early elements in that dialogue – in family and school – might be:

- *Sense of trust*   Trust towards oneself and towards others, as receiving and giving develops. Significant communiction does not occur until some relationship of trust is established.

- *Sense of autonomy*   A child needs the constant care, supervision and love of his parents; on the other hand, he needs to asset his will and stand over against his parents as a separate person. He needs to be part of others and distinct from them, to belong and yet to be self-sufficient.

- *Sense of initiative*   A child must find out what kind of person he is going to be. His search will be helped if he has been encouraged to develop a sense of initiative. It is the power that moves people to begin things.

- *Sense of industry*   Playing, schoolwork and membership of teams at school can develop a sense of industry. Vocational work – the principal contribution of adults – is central to personal life.

- *Sense of integrity*   Integrity means first learning to adhere to standards or values outside oneself. This gives life reference points other than self-interest. It aids the development of wholeness.

- *Sense of security*   People like and need a sense of security which comes from understanding where they stand in relation to the other significant people in their lives.

INDIVIDUALS AND INDIVIDUALISTS

Individuals are just particular persons. The word individual has gone through a revolution of meaning. Coming from the Latin *individuus*, indivisible, it was once used to emphasise that we are joined together: as individuals we are inseparable. Now it stresses the exact opposite, namely that each person is an indivisible whole, existing as a distinct entity.

The contemporary emphasis on our individuality, the total character that is peculiar to an individual and distinguishes him from others, has been fed by a number of cultural trends and tides in the West: religious, educational and artistic. In *Management and Morality* (1974)[12] and again in *Founding Fathers: The Puritans in England and America* (1984) I discussed the history of the concept of the individual and I shall not repeat myself here. One feature of Japan, a society immune from these influences until the middle of the last century, is the much greater prominence there of society, organisation and group and the relatively low development of the concept of individuality. That situation, of course, is changing as Western influences take effect.

An over-emphasis on the individual can be as harmful to effective team-work as an over-emphasis on the group. For it leads to *individualism* – the philosophy that the interests of the individual are or ought to be ethically paramount, coupled sometimes with the doctrine that all values, rights and duties originate in individuals. This in turn leads to a concentration on promoting the political and economic independence of the individual. The watchwords are individual initiative, action and interests. This ideology of individualism is based upon a half-truth: it ignores the other half of the picture, that we are all 'members one of another'. As Francis Quarles[13] expressed it:

No man is born unto himself alone
Who lives unto himself, he lives to none

These movement within our culture towards recognising the dignity of each person, and developing both our common and our peculiar characteristics through education, has made us all more self-conscious of our individuality. Sometimes that heightened awareness is accompanied by a sense of cosmic loneliness. Alexander Selkirk – the prototype of Robinson Crusoe – voiced that feeling in William Cowper's poem: 'I am out of humanity's reach, I must finish my journey alone'.

Most of us are not so out of love with humanity that we should deliberately choose to isolate ourselves from others. Some people do. For them freedom is necessary in order to be an individual. Therefore they are fleeing the constraints of group membership, mindless of its rewards.

Henry Thoreau, the American writer who took to living alone in the wilderness of a hundred years ago, wrote: 'Wherever a man goes, other men will pursue him and paw him with their dirty institutions, and if they can, will constrain him to belong to their desperate oddfellow society'.

The extreme individualist, in the first sense as one who advocates and practises individualism, is obviously going to find it difficult to work as a member of a team. For team membership involves a contract to put the interests of the whole team before one's own, at least for the duration of a task. If the group's interests conflict with his own – or any other individual's for that matter – he will invariably put the rights of the individual first. The natural tendency for communities and organisations peopled by such individualists is towards fragmentation. In the early colonial days of America, for example, such individualists were allowed to go and settle in what is now the state of Rhode Island, where they predictably made heavy weather of governing themselves.

Working groups, communities and organisations, however, should be able to accommodate individualists in the second sense of that word: those who pursue a markedly independent course in thought and action. For creative people – artists and scientists, inventors and leaders – tend to be individualists within this meaning of the word.

It is not easy to lead or manage individualists, nor is it easy for individualists to submit themselves to being managed or led by others. They are far more likely to respond to good leaders – leaders they respect and trust – than to being managed in a systematic, routine or bureaucratic way. They of all people need to be treated as individuals – the subject of the next section.

Apart from the way they are treated, what attracts the individualist into a working group and what sustains him while he is in it?

In order to answer the first question we must go back for a moment to the concept of reciprocity, the giving and receiving which expresses and builds up personality.

SHARING

Giving and receiving implies a two-fold model of relationship. In Fig. 5.1 the two people concerned are metaphorically gazing into each other's eyes:

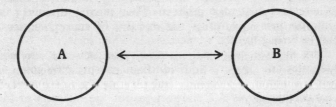

Fig. 5.1

But there is a third concept, which might be called *sharing*. The two people in Fig. 5.2 are metaphorically gazing together towards a third object or person. They see each other, so to speak, out of the corners of their eyes; they come closer together as they move towards the common object of interest:

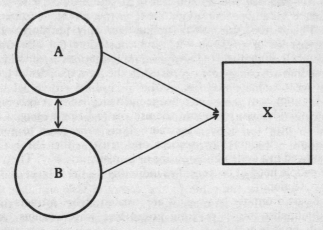

Fig. 5.2

Giving and receiving between A and B´still occurs in the three-fold model, but it happens within the context of the common interest, task or area of concern X. If you have a passion for stamp collecting, for example, you may give and receive gifts of specimens – or barter them with a fellow enthusiast in your stamp club, or you may simply swap ideas on how to conserve and display your collection.

Even the most devout individualist can therefore be drawn into the social life of co-operation when he discovers that someone else – perhaps an equally ardent individualist – shares his particular interest. This mental discovery of common ground is often the moment of conception for a lasting friendship.

If X has sufficient value for them, then, A and B may well be willing to accept a limit on their individual freedoms in order to pursue successfully and together the object of their common desire.

The first condition for free persons to co-operate is this perception of value in the common task. It has to be worthwhile. The second factor – the one that can sustain an individualist in a group or team – is the ability to internalise discipline: to transform the constraints that the common task and the need to work together impose into self-discipline. This seems to me the only way of reconciling two apparent opposites. For self-discipline implies constraint, but because it is self-imposed you remain free – no one is doing it to you. Hence Milton's exhortation: 'Love virtue, she alone is free'.

This virtue, this self-discipline, not only transforms the experience of social or technical constraints but also transcends their demands. The minimum limitations on individual freedom are commonly expressed in the form of codes of laws or rules, some unwritten. A self-disciplined individual will both fulfil and sometimes transcend these rules. A naturally courteous person, for example, will sometimes say more or do more than the conventions of etiquette or good manners require of him. He is seen to be free although he has in fact subjected himself to a demanding principle.

Can individualists work in groups and teams? Yes, provided they see sufficient value in the common task and that co-operative effort is more likely to produce results than individual effort. That rational argument needs to be won. But they will not sustain their place in working teams unless they are prepared to discipline themselves to accept – and perhaps go beyond – the standards of the group. Such self-discipline, however, carries an attractive bonus. For it maintains personal freedom, the reverse face of individuality.

ON TREATING PEOPLE AS INDIVIDUALS

We are all individuals, though not all of us are individualists. Groups and organisations that treat its members as individuals are more likely to be successful than those which treat them as a set of numbers. But what does the cry 'please, *please*, treat me as an individual' really mean?

The recognition that every person, like every situation, is unique is the foundation of the necessary attitude. There are naturally similarities between us – of needs, temperament, interest, habit, job, and so on – but in each of us the similarity is qualified in a peculiar way. You and I may both have a sense of humour, but it will be a different sense of humour, the differences apparent to both of us and our friends as we come to know each other well.

As a manager, you are like tens of thousands of other managers, and yet you are relatively different. That is, if you are to act and be acted upon in the most fruitful way, the best being drawn out from you and the best being given to you, you must regard yourself and be regarded by others in your individuality.

When regarded simply as a manager (or an operative) you become merely a specimen of a kind. One of the paradoxes of modern life is that while the claims of individuality are more frequently and more vociferously voiced than ever before, we are organising ourselves more busily along lines that suppress individuality. In one group after another we are being persuaded, cajoled, trapped or pressured into suppressing our initiative, judgement and responsibility. Many people are ceasing to have either power or significance except as a member of this group or that. We have compressed our complex individuality into the areas where we conform and resemble others.

Liberation from such incipient group or organisational tyranny only comes when the individual is recognised, grasped and accepted in his individuality as well as his humanity and personhood. That includes an appreciation of the unique contribution that *this* person can make both to common task and common life.

Exercise

Select any individual you know well and list the ways in which they *differ* from other persons under the following headings:

Temperament	Perception
Attitudes	Beliefs
Abilities	Motivation
Values	Skills
Knowledge	Character
Intelligence	Creativity
History	Background

It has been said that an adult has tens of thousands of beliefs, hundreds of attitudes, but only dozens of values. Do you agree?

Reflections of a cricket captain

Mike Brearley, one of England's most successful cricket captains, reflects here on the need to balance individual and group interest in the team. How do you build a team of individualists?

Cricket is a team game, but as such it is unusual in being made up of intensely individual duels. Personal interest may conflict with that of the team: you may feel exhausted, and yet have to bowl, you may be required to sacrifice your wicket going for quick runs. And these conflicting tensions can easily give rise to the occupational vice of cricket – selfishness.

The drive for personal success is vital to the team. Without it, a player can fail to value himself, and assume a diffidence which harms the team. He might, for example, under-rate the importance to his confidence – and thus to the team's long-term interest – of his occupying the crease for hours, however boringly, in a search for form. And I have seen a whole side in flight from selfishness, with batsmen competing to find more ridiculous ways of getting themselves out in order to prove that they weren't selfish.

It is the captain's job to coax the happy blend of self-interest and team interest from his players, influencing the balance between individual and group. Thus he enables the group to create and sustain its identity without a deadening uniformity, and to enable the individuals to express themselves as fully as possible without damaging the interest of the whole.

Ian Botham, Brearley's successor as Captain of the England Cricket XI, said of him: 'There is something about the man. He reads me like a book. He knows what I am thinking and gets the best out of me'. It is this ability to understand each individual – each part that makes up the whole – that made Brearley such an outstanding leader.

POINTS TO PONDER

An individual is a particular person. Being fully a person means that he or she is capable of giving and receiving. We have notions of what is fair, namely an equivalence in this mutual exchange. But, possessed of the human spirit, we can transcend these moral ideas of justice in personal relationships.

We give according to our unique pattern of talents, abilities or gifts. Slowly we discover what they are. But we should be nothing if others did not receive our gifts. Where would Mozart be if no musicians gave him their skills or no audiences gave him their attention?

Achieving a balance between the interests and self-expression of each individual on the one hand and of the group on the other, is one of the most challenging tasks of leaders. It is best done by reference to the third dimension – the common task. For it is the value of that task which draws us together and underpins our unity.

Your attitudes are more fundamental to your success in teambuilding than any skills or techniques. They stem from your values. Explore your values and keep them in good repair.

Let us rejoice in our individuality, but let us be sure that we develop it for the benefit of others

6 Three interlocking needs in group life

Preview of Chapter Six

- What needs are present in the life of every group?
- Needs and leadership functions
- Some implications
- Points to ponder

'A picture is worth a thousand words', says the proverb. In this chapter I want to pull together with the help of a picture – the three circles – the threads of the preceding five chapters.

In my previous books on leadership I have advanced one general theory about working groups and organisations. Apart from being the only general theory in the field it has proved extremely fruitful as the basis for leadership training. More than one million managers have now been through courses based upon it.

This theory begins with the proposition that all groups (like persons) are individuals. Even groups in the same organisation develop after a time what Lord Attlee referring to British cabinets called 'a group personality'. For that reason what works in one group may not work in another. But groups share certain common needs. In this chapter we shall explore those needs and their implications for teams and leaders.

WHAT NEEDS ARE PRESENT IN THE LIFE OF EVERY GROUP?

The needs of the group can be summarised as follows:

Task

The need to accomplish something – build a house, sing an anthem, determine a budget, plan a conference, solve a problem, climb a mountain. The need of the group is to try to accomplish this task. So long as this task remains undone, there will be a tension in the group and an urge to complete the task. The task is *what* the group is talking about or working on. The task is usually seen in terms of *things* rather than people.

Group

The need to develop and maintain working relationships among the members so that the group task can be accomplished. This is called the maintenance need of the group. Maintenance refers primarily to *people* and their relationships with each other. It concerns *how* people relate to each other as they work at the group task. Unless members listen to each other, for example, and try to build upon each other's suggestions it will be very difficult, and often impossible, for the group to accomplish its task. Yet maintenance is frequently neglected in groups. How long would a fleet of jet airliners be able to operate if they were not serviced, refuelled and otherwise maintained?

Individual

The needs of individuals come with them into groups. People work in groups not only because of interest in the task to be accomplished but also because membership of groups fulfils their various needs.

Why do people work in the first place? They work because they are hungry, they are thirsty and they need somewhere to sleep. Even today, when we use money as a means of exchange, most of our salary goes in satisfying those basic needs. But a satisfied need ceases to motivate. Once you have enough food and drink, once you have a house, other needs rise up in the human heart. You become interested in a pension, job security and safety of work. If those security needs are satisfied by good company policy and through the welfare state, people do not then turn round and say 'Thank you, we are now fully satisfied'. Instead they discover other areas of need bubbling up within them: the quality of relationships in working life; respect from others and self-respect; and then the need for 'self-actualisation', a fulfilment of one's potential by growth. The needs for physical satisfaction and security are stronger and more deep-rooted; if they are threatened then we jump back and defend them. The needs for self-esteem, the respect of others and self-fulfilment are weaker, but they are more distinctively human.

If such needs can be met *along with* and not *at the expense of* the group task and maintenance needs, then the group will tend to be more effective.

As you will see from the diagram (Fig. 6.1), the circles overlap. If you achieve the common task the effects will flow into the group circle and help to create a sense of unity. And they will also influence the individual circle. In fact you can work round the diagram. If you have a good group, for example, you are more likely to achieve the task. If the individuals concerned are fully involved and motivated, then they are going to give much more to the task and much more to the group. By contrast, if you imagine a black circle totally eclipsing the task circle that would symbolise a total failure of the task area. You would then have taken quite a chunk out of the group area, and a similar one out of the individual circle too. If you could put that black circle over the group

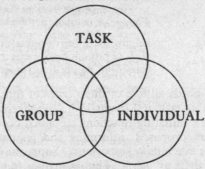

Fig. 6.1   Three Areas of Need

maintenance area, then again it would show that lack of group cohesiveness will affect the other two circles.

NEEDS AND LEADERSHIP FUNCTIONS

In order that the task and maintenance needs should be met, certain *functions* have to be performed. A function is what you do as opposed to a quality or trait.

In Chapter 4 I listed the 'roles' or functions introduced by Benne and Sheats in the late 1940s. Observers in Group Dynamics training laboratories found these rather long; moreover we found it difficult to use two separate forms at once. Therefore various efforts were made to produce a composite list.

One such working categorisation, suggested by Gibb and Gibb,[14] influenced my subsequent efforts. They indicated five broad categories of leadership functions:

Initiating:	keeping the group action moving, or getting it going (for example, suggesting action step, pointing out goal, proposing procedure, clarifying)
Regulating:	influencing the direction and tempo of the group's work (for example, summarising, pointing out time limits, restating goal)
Informing:	bringing information or opinion to the group
Supporting:	creating an emotional climate which holds group together, makes it easy for members to contribute to work on the task (for example, harmonising, relieving tension, voicing group feeling, encouraging)
Evaluating:	helping the group to evaluate its decisions, goals or procedures (for example, testing for consensus, noting group process)

A group needs all five of these types of function if it is to accomplish its task and maintain its cohesiveness. Early in a group's work initiating functions are much needed. Later, as solutions are proposed, informing and regulating functions may assume much more importance. Supporting functions are needed all the way along. The evaluating function becomes especially relevant as the group nears the end of its work.

Group work will be effective, then, to the degree that needed group functions are supplied at the time they are needed.

SOME IMPLICATIONS

Sooner or later all three kinds of needs present in every group must be met to some extent in order to achieve effectiveness and satisfaction. When needed functions are missing, group progress is slow and uneven.

This does *not* imply that at every moment exactly one third of the group's attention and energy should be devoted to each of these three kinds of needs. Over a period of time there may be great fluctuations in the amount of group attention and energy directed to any one of these needs. The amount of energy to be allocated depends upon the ability of the members to diagnose which of the three needs is most pressing at every moment, and their ability to meet this perceived need.

The performing of one function may help to meet two or even three needs simultaneously.

Most people usually have preferences for providing one or another function most often, such as the inveterate summariser. Hence the tendency to use the word 'role' in the context of group life. But most people can at least potentially make more than one functional contribution.

POINTS TO PONDER

Always bear in mind the three-circles model. It is a simple sketchmap of working group life. If and when a group bogs down, look for a needed but missing function, and then perform it or encourage someone else to perform it.

Through training (which includes observation and practice) you can learn to perform skilfully a wide variety of useful member functions.

Skill is technique that has been mastered to the point where you do not have to think about it. In working groups it consists of knowing *what* to say and do, *when*, and *how*.

The skilfulness of your participation is to be judged more by its *effect* upon the group than by your own intentions.

Acquiring skill is learning to bring behaviour into line with your intentions

7 Group processes

Process issues, you may recall, revolve around the underlying ways in which a group works. Again, to repeat an earlier point, it is not the same as group maintenance. In this and the following chapter I shall draw out some more lessons about group processes which are relevant to teamwork today.

In order to clothe the rather nebulous concept of process I have chosen three examples: responses to authority, response to frustration and decision-making procedures. These are obviously not directly connected with each other. Taken together, however, they can take us some steps further in understanding more fully what goes on in groups.

In each section you should bear in mind the Group Dynamics provenance for these ideas. But I have selected these particular instances of group process because I have experienced them many times in working groups and I have found the work of psychologists here illuminating rather than obfuscating.

PROCEDURES

All groups need to use some procedures – ways of working – to get things done. In formal business meetings we are accustomed to a set of rules or procedures. Informal groups usually use less rigid procedures. The choice of procedures has a direct effect on such other aspects of group life as atmosphere, participation and cohesion. Choosing procedures that are appropriate to the situation and the work to be done may require a degree of flexibility and inventiveness by a group.

CHECKLIST

- How does the group determine its practices or agenda?
- How does it make decisions – by vote, silent assent, consensus?
- How does it discover and make use of the resources of its members?
- How does the work of various members, subgroups and activities get co-ordinated?
- How does it evaluate its work?

DECISION MAKING

Group processes revolve around the core of decision making. How are decisions made? Or do they just happen? That is a central issue for groups.

Take the case of a group of doctors working together in a primary health care team in Bristol. There are four doctors together with district nurses and health visitors making up this team. The senior partner is a woman aged 51, and the other doctors – all men – are aged 29, 32 and 35. At one meeting the younger doctors proposed that if disagreements arose about matters concerning the group practice, decisions should be taken by vote. The senior partner put her foot down and insisted that decisions should be by consensus. Do you think she was right to do so?

Decisions occur – or do not, as the case may be – by a variety of methods. Here you will see group processes at work in the following ways:

- *Apathy*

  Nobody is sufficiently interested or concerned to get the group to operate, that is, deciding not to decide by tacit agreement.

- *Plops*

  A decision suggested by an individual to which there is no response. Plopping often occurs in a new group confronted by many problems; in a group where a number of the members have fairly equal status; when a member is overly aggressive; when a member has difficulty in articulating.

- *Self-authorised decisions*

  A decision made by an individual who assumes authority to do so. When such a decision is proposed, the group as a whole often finds it easier to accept than reject, even though some individuals may not be in agreement. The decision is thus by default.

- *Pairing*

  A decision made by two members of the group joining forces. Such 'hand-clasping' sometimes emerges so suddenly that it catches the other members of the group off guard and at the same time presents them with another problem (how to deal with the two people at once).

- *Topic-jumping*

  A decision to cut short by the inappropriate intrusion of another topic. Topic-jumping confuses the issue confronting the group and thus changes the nature of the decision.

- *Minority group*

  A decision agreed upon in advance by several members of the group. Cliques are present in almost every group, and their pre-arranged decision may be very good. But the effect of collusion can be to destroy group cohesiveness and a sense of trust.

- *Majority views*

  A decision made by some form of voting. The traditional procedure of taking a vote often seems to be the only way in which to reach a decision under the given circumstances. Nonetheless the minority may remain against the decision despite the vote and therefore not likely to act on it.

- *Does anyone
  disagree?*

A decision made by pressure not to disagree. When confronted by such a question, several persons who really disagree strongly or who have not had opportunity to express their opinion on the issue, might show real reluctance to voice opposition with no apparent support.

Note that Fig. 7.1 on decision making in groups includes *true consensus* and *false consensus*. In the latter everyone *appears* to agree but when the decision is acted upon each member seems to have different ideas about the decision or to have reserved the right not to implement it. Some members may have only pretended to agree in the first place, hoping the matter would be forgotten or that the decision could subsequently be fudged.

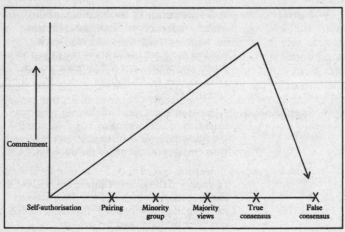

Fig. 7.1   Ways of Reaching a Decision

True consensus is not always possible even if it is normally desirable, because it can be very time-consuming. It occurs when communcation has been sufficiently open for all to feel they have had a fair chance to influence decision and the 'feeling of the meeting' emerges without voting. The following definition is worth bearing in mind:

When alternatives have been debated thoroughly by the group and everyone is prepared to accept that in the circumstances one particular solution is the best way forward, even though it might not be *every* person's preferred solution.

The most important test is that everyone is prepared to *act* as though it was their preferred solution.

RESPONSES TO AUTHORITY

Not all the processes at work below the surface – or on it – in group life are concerned with making decisions or constitute procedures for tackling common goals. Under the umbrella of group processes we can look at two recurring patterns in group life: the different responses to the leader's authority and the tendency of groups to withdraw or 'take flight' when faced with difficulty.

The T-group began with the trainer asking the group to 'become a group' and then sitting back, apparently leaving them to their own devices.

This overt behaviour – apparently a complete abdication from the leadership role – sparked off several reactions in groups which in time became fairly predictable. Although conditioned and sharpened by the T-group environment they are latent in all of us and you will have experienced some of them in daily life at work in certain situations. The first pair, for example, would be recognised by most of us in our family roles as children and parents:

Dependency   Members look to others to tell them what to do. They are completely dependent upon the 'authority figure' and are lost without him.

Counterdependency Members resist authority, especially from the leader. They are hostile to any attempt to curtail their freedom. 'What right have you got to tell me what to do?'.

The *dependency* and *counterdependency* phases we go through as children in regard to our parents and teachers can get fixed. There are adults who carry around with them these latent attitudes towards those in authority.

The dependent person clearly needs to be nurtured – coaxed, counselled and coached – into taking a less dependent stance in regard to authority. It is not easy because the pattern of dependency can be stamped on a person's nature by parents and teachers.

In dealing with counterdependence it is important to realise first that these hostile, frustrated feelings are not being directed at you personally. They are often the by-product left in the human soul of over-dominant parents or autocratic teachers. In weaning someone from counterdependency you should not parade your authority; your legitimate authority should stem from your knowledge and personality.

In emerging from these two states (and counterdependency can be the flipside of dependency) we have to go through the stage of *independence*. The independent person is neither dependent nor counterdependent to a leader. The adjective carries good overtones of autonomy and freedom.

Independence can also mean: 'I am going to have nothing to do with you'. In this case the person severs himself from the offending source of authority, if need be by force or flight. This may be necessary if that authority has tried to keep you in leading-strings or is authoritarian in its behaviour. Otherwise independence is a natural phase of growing up.

Yet it is not the end of the story. For independence in the second sense contravenes the elementary principle of reciprocity: that we are made for, and made in, a fundamental process of giving and receiving. The natural end of our striving, then, is the state of *interdependence*, the social commerce of free and equal individuals who accept that their skills, natures and needs are complementary.

FIGHT AND FLIGHT

When faced with a difficulty, especially one that is threatening, humans can either stand their ground and fight or they can take flight. This behaviour can be categorised as follows:

Fighting and dominating	Disagreeing; asserting personal dominance; attacking whatever is believed to be responsible for the cause of stress. It is common, for example, to blame others – individuals, groups, institutions, ideas.
Flight and withdrawal	Staying out of discussion; day-dreaming; sulking; running away physically or psychologically.
Pairing	In pairing, individuals seek reassurance from other individuals about their feelings of anxiety or discomfort.

But sometimes the whole group may take a fighting stance. Doubtless you can think of groups who have become belligerent. What is not so obvious, however, is when a group is *taking flight* in a psychological way from a dangerous area.

You may notice symptoms include a higher degree of rather artificial play acting or 'larking about'. Nervous humour and jokes are often symptoms of tension, for laughter is a safety valve. This is why groups often laugh at jokes or remarks that are not really funny.

An intriguing method of group flight occurs when the discussion shifts from the particular to the *general* – and stays there. It can be a form of flight, for example, to discuss the 'problem of leadership today' rather than tackle the central issue in the group, which is: 'You, Jack, are not giving us any leadership'.

It is of course not always true that groups who are talking in general or theoretical terms are evading some problem within their own life. Sometimes their very reason for being there is to explore such areas in an intellectual fashion. But you should be able to judge when it is flight into the general or abstract. As a form of veering away mentally from a problem or difficulty they should be tackling, it can afflict all groups in all places.

DEFENCE MECHANISMS

The flight into abstract or general discourse is an example of a largely unconscious group response (although a cunning member may manipulate the discussion in that direction if he wants no decision to be taken). But individuals also develop unconscious responses to anxiety-making situations. Some of them get 'institutionalised' in their psychological make-up. These can sometimes help to explain why a person may be acting or reacting in a certain way.

One important group are the so-called defence mechanisms. The identification of them was one of the more useful outcomes of Sigmund Freud's work. Defence mechanisms, he believed, are employed by individuals to reduce or overcome anxiety. They provide some insights into human behaviour in groups.

Displacement:	for example, where a subordinate is annoyed at his boss and punishes his own subordinates or some other person
Repression:	a process by which unacceptable desires or impulses are excluded from consciousness and left to operate in the unconscious, for example, where an individual blocks out or represses an unpleasant experience
Regression:	reversion to an earlier mental or behavioural level, for example, when an adult behaves in a childish fashion
Over-reaction:	for example, becoming excessively bureaucratic or rule-abiding
Projection:	the act of externalising or objectifying what is primarily subjective, for example, projecting one's own thoughts or desires onto others
Fixation:	an obsessive or unhealthy preoccupation or attachment, for example, a persistent concentration on a supposed threat or enemy
Sublimation:	directing the energy of (an impulse) from its primitive aim to one that is ethically or culturally higher; for example, a naturally aggressive person who becomes an attacking hockey centre forward

Fig. 7.2   Some Depth Mind Strategies

It is unwise to play the role of amateur psychologist if you are a leader or manager, for a little learning is a dangerous thing. But Freud's categories can sometimes throw light on the thought-processes or behaviour of individuals in relationships. It may be, too, that groups that have been together for a time will also develop their own defence mechanisms. It also may displace, repress, over-react, project and form fixations.

In other words, these can be group as well as individual phenomena. As always, the price of freedom is eternal vigilance.

POINTS TO PONDER

With practice of observation, using this book as a guide, you should be able to distinguish between the *content* of group discussion and the *process* of group life. Look below the surface and ask yourself 'what is going on here'.

Decisions will be influenced by group or individual processes that are not immediately apparent. Improved decision making will emerge from a clearer understanding of these pressures and allowing for their effects. Self-awareness is the key.

Attitudes to authority in general – dependence and counter-dependence – can influence the way that group members respond to your leadership. Keep calm. Conduct yourself so as to make it easier for the group and each individual within it to move towards *interdependence* – with you and each other.

Escapism into dreams or fantasy is no bad thing sometimes – we all do it. But a group that takes flight from the 'here and now' into abstractions, sustained endlessly by psychological filibustering, is never likely to be effective.

Consensus is a valuable goal in decision making. Where members know each other well, share values and can spend time in discussion together, it should be the rule. But where these factors are not present it is not always possible for a leader to find it.

By understanding what goes on within groups you can learn to work with the grain rather than against it.

8 Groups within groups

Many groups run into trouble because they ignore the fact that as a group they are part of a wider organisation. They may work happily and well as a close knit team, but somehow their efforts are not supported by other parts of the organisation. The group may even come under attack. It has ignored the principle of always seeing one's group as part of a larger whole. That should start within the group itself and work upwards and outwards.

If you put a group – say of about ten to fifteen people in a face-to-face relationship with each other – under a meta-phorical microscope you will find that it is made up of actual or potential subgroups, like an atom disclosing neutrons and other sub-atomic particles. These can be at odds with each other.

Conversely, if you stand back a mile and look at the same group through a metaphorical telescope you will see that it is one of a cluster of groups forming part of a larger organisation or community. Go back two or three miles and your telescope will reveal that the organisation in turn is part of a galaxy of like-sized or related organisations. If you could move far enough away and use a radio telescope, your organisation would appear as a mere dot on the screen, a speck in the universe of world society streaming past in light years of time.

This chapter, while continuing to pursue the theme of *intra*group relations by looking at subgroups, will focus on the study of conflict and harmony *between* groups. Just as no individual exists in isolation so no group functions by itself. So great is the *inter-dependence of groups* today that events in one are invariably transmitted to others, producing either harmony or discord in them.

SUBGROUPS

Each group contains actual or potential subgroups. These often reflect membership of other groups, for example, fathers, mothers, trades unionists, golfers, managers, car drivers, or they may be clusters of like-minded individuals.

For in every group the participants tend very soon to begin to identify certain individuals that they like more than other members, and others they like less. These subtle relationships of friendship and antipathy have an important influence on the group's activities. There is some research, for example, that suggests that people tend to agree with people they like and disagree with people they dislike. In Fig. 8.1 we see the subgroups which exist within a group of chartered accountants.

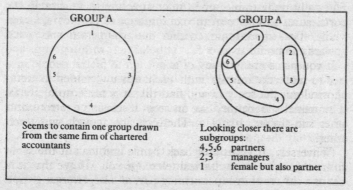

Fig. 8.1   The Audit Group

During any one day a person may move between a number of these groups. They are *informal* groupings as opposed to the *formal* groups – such as committees, working parties and project groups – established as part of the organisational structure or by a formal act of authority.

Exercise

Can you identify the subgroups in your own primary work group? What are their principal distinguishing characteristics?

THE EFFECTS OF INTERGROUP CONFLICT

Experience of life shows us that individuals, because they have differing goals, needs, ways of looking at the world and so on, often find themselves in conflict with others. The more the individual defines the situation as one in which he can only gain his goals at the expense of others, the more conflict is likely. The more he defines the situation as one in which it is possible for all to reach their goals, the more co-operation is likely.

Conflict in the sense of contrast of ideas is not undesirable; only through expression of difference can good problem-solving take place. Contrast can lead to clarification, progress or seeing a way forward. Expecting everyone to agree is as unrealistic as assuming that no agreement is possible. But conflict is to be avoided, chiefly because it diverts the activity of a group from getting on with their job. It becomes especially undesirable when it is so severe as to disable the participants and prevent the continuation of problem-solving.

In order to examine conflict and co-operation between groups it is useful to look first at behaviour within groups and consequent characteristics.

The more the inter-group situation is understood in terms of win/lose, the more likely you will see some hostile effects. The more it is defined as making decisions or overcoming problems the less likely these effects are, though they never completely disappear.

When two are competing together in training situations the following sorts of behaviour are typical. They represent changes of relationship *within the group* and *between groups*.

Remember, however, that these are only tendencies. These behaviours do not invariably occur.

Within the groups:

- *Cohesiveness* — Each group pulls in closer together; it sees the other as the enemy, so loyalty to the group increases. Suddenly we become a 'good group' and forget our internal difficulties.

- *Perceptions* — Perception becomes distorted; each group sees only the best in itself and the worst in the other. Feeling that the group is inherently good increases. A filter or screen is put up for incoming information.

- *Territorial imperative* — The group feels it owns and must guard certain territory for example, its rooms. It acts also to protect territory in the wider sense, for example, 'We are responsible for customer service, not you'.

- *Conformity* — Each group expects or even demands more conformity from its members and accepts more control from its leaders. There is much more emphasis upon unity at all costs.

- *Atmosphere* — This changes high to low concern about the task as more and more effort is put into maintaining the group.

- *Structure* — More structure is introduced, sometimes reflecting interests of powerful subgroups or revealing cleavages between them.

The general tendencies, then, are for each group to close ranks, to become more cohesive, and to place a much higher value on itself than upon the other group. The latter becomes the enemy, the implicit or explicit threat to one's own group. Insecurity lurks below the surface of all our dealings with each other. It is relatively easy to mobilise this sense of insecurity in order to unite a group in the face of a common threat. Whether it is wise to do so is another matter. To me there is all the difference in the world between a common threat which is an external, real one, and a group that is at least in theory on your own side.

Between the groups:

- *Hostility*   Members become hostile towards the other group. These hostile attitudes can erupt into various forms of aggressive rhetoric and behaviour. Bad stereotypes are formed of the other group, based on the worst assumptions about their motives.

- *Communication*   Interaction slackens and communication decreases: the group does not want to see the other. Words and non-verbal behaviour are interpreted in ways which support the group's own position. Members do not listen to the 'adversary'; they hear only that which supports their own position. They may even attack points of the adversary's position which are in fact already accepted in their own group.

- *Mistrust*   The less the two groups communicate, the more their meanings are distorted by interpretations made in the context of presuppositions and prejudices. Mutual understanding drops to zero. Members mistrust the other group (and its representatives). There is a strong emphasis on politics rather than solving the problem on its merits.

The relations between two groups caught in this vicious spiral can only deteriorate rapidly. Mistrust creates less and worse communication, which in turn breeds more mistrust.

When two (or more) groups are faced with a joint problem they may try to solve it in isolation from each other, they may be forced together by a directive from senior management or one group may win and 'beat' the other, possibly leaving the losing group very demoralised. By assuming that a real solution is wanted which satisfies both groups, then some kind of joint problem-solving process must take place.

As loyalty to our own group is important to all of us, it follows that inter-group conflict is likely to be especially acute. We cannot direct our hostile feelings within our own groups very strongly: to do so would invite rejection. But hostility directed outward not only relieves us, but strengthens our membership in our own group. Thus any inter-group problem-solving situation is likely to contain hostility, along with genuine attempts at co-operation.

If groups perceive themselves to be in a Win/Lose situation they will interpret the subsequent results of their transactions in those categories.

What happens to winners	*What happens to losers*
• Become more cohesive	• Group fragments, fights, reorganises.
• Release of tension	• Increase in tension; they are ready to dig harder. May end up 'lean and hungry'.
• More self-congratulation and play; less fighting spirit	• Scapegoating – often own leaders and organisations are blamed.
• May become less productive	• May blame themselves and become depressed if 'winning' seems impossible in the future.
• May end up complacent: 'fat and happy'	• The group can learn a lot about itself.

Victory or defeat therefore can change perceptions. For the 'winners' it reinforces their picture of themselves and therefore paradoxically makes it harder for them to change and *remain* winners. Defeat can shatter the self-image of a group. But that may release them to consider much more radical change.

The American Congress at work

Congress is a mad-house of committees and sub-committees. All congressmen want to be special for the folks back home, so they want to run something. There are 435 members of the House of Representatives and 100 Senators: 202 of them are in charge of something, however small.

Committees have their own will for life, their own struggle for status nd recognition. Committees are places where political staffers pursue their esoteric Capitol Hill careers. Committees consequently spend a good deal of time in battle with other committees. The staffs continually get larger and more cumbersome. This is democracy by bureaucracy.

Many disputes are territorial. Committee One often does not know what Committee Two is doing. Opposite resolutions can emerge on the same subject. The same witnesses can be called before two committees to discuss the same issue. Often, events grind on interminably because senators and representatives are determined to say something that will get them on the evening news back home. Democracy must be seen to be done, and votes must be got.

Christopher Thomas, *The Times* (30.1.85)

TRANSACTIONS BETWEEN GROUPS

In order to break out of their separate boxes, members of the two groups – Group A and Group B – will need to cross the *boundaries* they have each established around themselves.

One familiar method is to send an 'ambassador' to talk to the other group. We can represent that situation visually, as in Fig. 8.2.

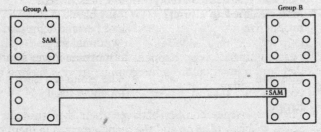

Fig. 8.2

Sam has been appointed as a representative of Group A to go and confer with Group B. He has to operate, temporarily at least, as a member of two groups.

Moreover, Group A has to work with one person short, while Group B now has an extra person.

Group B may feel on its guard. Sam will be received cautiously. For he comes from Group A, and Group B already has a picture of what Group A is like. Sam's conduct of himself may confirm these ideas. Alternatively, meeting Sam and hearing what he has to say may lead Group B to modify its perception of Group A.

If Group B's image of Group A is deeply entrenched it is unlikely that Sam's behaviour will be able to shift them. That is also true in reverse. If Sam's (Group A) view of Group B is very strong, then whatever Group B actually do or say when he meets them will not affect his opinion of them.

Meanwhile Group A continues in being. Despite his absence Sam still has influence within it. 'What would Sam say to that if he was here?' Indeed thinking about Sam, and how he is getting on with Group B, could prove to be a distraction for Group A from the task in hand.

After Sam's return Group A may well have to deal with someone who has differing views from it, that is views which he has accepted in debate with Group B and now seeks to import into his own group.

Meanwhile, back in Group B, they are wondering how Sam is getting on, what he thought of them, and so on.

Exercise

How have you felt when representing a group?
Cautious and guarded? Stereotyped and pressurised?
Independent? Tied to a brief?

We can summarise what happens to representatives sent to the other group in situations where competition is verging on the brink of conflict:

- They experience conflict between their own strategies, goals, wishes and so on and the mandate given to them by their group.

- There is tension resulting from being responsible for their group's success or failure.

- They are seen as a 'hero' if their own group wins; and as a 'traitor' if they lose.

If judges, arbitrators or 'third parties' are drawn from the groups they also experience similar stresses. The role of the 'middleman' is never easy, but it is made severe if you are a member of one of the two or more groups in contention. The predicament of such arbitrators may be summarised thus:

- They find it hard to divorce themselves from their group or origin and are unable to be neutral.

- They experience conflict between loyalty to their own group and the role of 'judge'.

- They are seen as 'biased' by losing group; they are praised by the winners.

Effects like those described are familiar enough. We can see them both within organisations and between organisations, within communities and nations, and between nations. A common cause in organisations is an over-emphasis upon competition rather than co-operation, leading to hostility, suspicion, misunderstanding, lack of trust, 'closing ranks' under assault and finally breaking off all communication. An understanding of how this vicious circle of interactions occurs is an aid if you want to break into the vicious spiral before it strangles the organisation.

The key step in resolving this kind of negative competition is to find a common or 'superordinate' goal – one which both (or all) groups accept as essential to reach, and which both can reach together. Such a goal is more likely to be a more general and longer-term aim rather than a highly specific or concrete short-term objective. How can things be worked that *both* groups get what they want?

THE GROUP'S RELATIONSHIP WITH ITS ENVIRONMENT

We have considered the dire consequences when two groups are working against each other rather than with each other. As they polarise it becomes increasingly difficult to reconcile them. Any original issues are forgotten and it becomes a matter of who is going to win and who is going to lose. Many an industrial strike follows that unfruitful path.

But such disorders should never have happened if like individuals kept to Dr Samuel Johnson's injunction to keep their friendship in good repair. Otherwise its contribution to the overall aims and objectives may not be understood and accepted; it may even come under fire and, eventually, the threat of disbandment. Prevention of this state of affairs is better than cure.

Examples of problems which are symptoms of this *malaise* of poor or indistinct relationships of the group with the rest of the organisation include:

- The output of the group's work may not be seen as appropriate, relevant or of the right quality

- The group can't obtain the resources it needs or the decisions it wants

- The group fails to recognise resources available to it from outside the group

- It doesn't receive the right quality or quantity of information it needs to do its job

- It is attacked because it seems a close-knit and effective group and as such is threatening to other groups or individuals

- There is conflict within the group because individual members have split loyalties (to the group and to other parts of the organisation) which have not been recognised and discussed)

Such problems are usually caused because there is a mismatch in expectations between the group and the various individuals and bits of the organisation with which it interacts.

An important job for any group is to establish good working relationships within the organisation as a whole. These may involve individuals, groups or 'systems' (for example, the planning system, the development system).

Described below is a systematic but simple way of establishing what the nature of these relationships needs to be, and whether any work needs to be done by the group to improve them.

CHECKLIST: HOW TO MANAGE INTERGROUP RELATIONSHIPS

1 What are the key boundaries? Make a list of those other groups that are important to it in fulfilling its purpose, aims and objectives. In a multi-functional group include group members departments.

2   What expectations or demands does each of those groups have of
    our group?
    What expectations or demands does the group have in return?

3   What is the nature of the work relationship required across the
    boundary to meet both sets of expectations? For example:
    information giving/receiving
    influencing/recommending
    giving/receiving a service
    reporting
    monitoring

4   How well is the relationship working across that boundary
    currently?
    – Is the group responding adequately to the demands and
      expectations on it?
    – Is the interface fulfilling the requirements the group has of it?
    – Is there a mismatch of expectations?

5   What *work* needs to be done to put things on a sounder footing?
    Which group members should be responsible for taking the
    necessary action?

Not only will this type of analysis help the group ensure it
relates effectively to the wider organisation, but, if done
jointly by the group, it also helps to build group identity
through a joint understanding of the environment in which it
will have to operate.

ON COMPETITION AND CO-OPERATION

Competition and co-operation have been mentioned more than
once in this book. There is considerable confusion about the
relation between these two states or activities and it is essential
to try to think clearly about them. Here is my philosophy of
competition and co-operation[15].

In many situations, not all, a leader or group is faced with
an apparent choice between competing or co-operating with
others. It is a decision to vie against others or to show a
willingness and ability to work with them.

This appears to be an either/or decision. But it is worth
thinking it through more carefully, not least in order to avoid
unnecessary intergroup conflict. It is also important to be clear
about the part which competition can play in teambuilding
and team maintenance.

The first principle is that competition is not antithetically opposed to co-operation. In other words, to have more of one does not mean that we must necessarily have less of the other. The true alternative to competition in economics, for example, is not co-operation but monopoly.

A second principle is that fair and open competition, though understandably uninviting to reluctant, sluggish or incompetent competitors, is one of the surest means known to us of maintaining and raising standards in whatever it may be that the competitors are trying to produce, achieve or sell.

The concept of competition essentially involves comparisons with others in terms of better or worse performance. These comparisons are essentially relative. There is no connection in a competition to the position of the competitor on any absolute scale of merit. It is quite possible to get ahead of the competition but still be low on an absolute scale of merit in that field. The reverse is also true. Britain's economy, for example, was growing gradually in the 1960s and 1970s but the country was slipping down most of the league tables of performance among the industrialised nations.

Competition therefore involves a striving by every competitor to do better than all the rest; it is concerned with relative positions between the competitors rather than their place on some scale of standards. So competition can be pursued to utter exclusion of such concerns as doing better than one's own last performance on the appropriate scale of merit or of helping others to better their own performances in this way.

But competition, though concerned with relative achievement, is often the practically necessary condition for promoting or securing the absolutely better. It is perfectly possible for people engaged in competition to be aware of this factor and to be as much directed at absolute standards – such as excellence – as doing better than the opposition.

There are indeed occasions when a choice has to be made between the alternatives of competition and co-operation. Two firms bidding for an international contract to build a suspension bridge may have to choose between submitting competitive tenders or forming a consortium and putting in just one tender, thereby hoping to win the order against foreign competition. Thus competition and co-operation can exist in the same universe.

This coexistence is exemplified by the fact that competition is often between two teams. No team is going to do well if its members do not co-operate. Even in individual contests a modicum of co-operation is necessary. If you are playing tennis against an opponent he has to co-operate to the extent of agreeing to play and give you a game, as well as turning up at the right time and place. All team games call for this element of co-operation *between* teams as well as *within* them.

Competition, then, is one of the most effective incentives towards achieving higher levels of performance. Co-operation is essential for getting things done. Fortunately they are not always and everywhere exclusive and incompatible alternatives.

It follows that a leader should handle competition – within the group or between groups within his organisation – extremely carefully. Otherwise the kind of interpersonal and intergroup rivalries and changes in attitude described elsewhere in this chapter will overtake him. For competition for outside prizes or scarce resources internal to the competition is bound to engage people's emotions. 'Winning isn't everything', said one American football coach, 'but losing ain't anything'. If contest is stressed too much then the sole object becomes only to better the competition. And competitive desires are especially liable to frustration in a way that the desire to do better than your last performance is not. For if all salesmen in a group are competing hard to be Top Salesman of the Year all but one are going to be disappointed.

Within groups or organisations competition should be regarded much as a game, but a game with a serious object: to raise the standards of all concerned towards a common level of excellence. Competition outside the organisation, with others vying in the same field, also serves the same purpose of producing goods and services at best value for money. For leaders who want to change their organisations or groups for the better, a useful first objective is to get to the top of the league table of effective competitors. Even then the summit of excellence will still lie ahead, shrouded in mist.

There will be occasions, however, when a leader of an organisation will want co-operation with other organisations in that field: in, say, an approach to government. This is the role of trade associations and the like. But co-operation should never be used to introduce unfair advantages, such as a secret agreement by a 'ring' of dealers before an auction. Co-operation between organisations who are also normally competitors should be such as to enhance the standing of the industry as a whole, relative to other industries, in the public mind.

The purpose is better performance – to do better today than you did yesterday, and to do better tomorrow than you are doing today. Co-operation and competition both have essential parts to play in that endless quest.

POINTS TO PONDER

Groups exist within groups. Become aware of these sub-groupings. They may indicate the potential cracks in the team.

Groups on the same side are often like islands addressing each other across a sea of misunderstanding. As a leader it is your job to develop teamwork *between* groups as well as within them.

Winning and losing are imposters. Winning brings a whole set of new problems for a group, while losing may be a blessing in disguise.

Competition sharpens skills but they can only be used effectively in co-operation with others.

Part Two
BUILDING AND MAINTAINING HIGH-PERFORMANCE TEAMS

'There are four people who should be the hub of the wheel in my factory', said Michael Dix, production director of a factory making shoes. 'The problem is that the organisational structure makes them look like four separate apples hanging on a tree. The chart doesn't say that they have to be a team but that is what this business requires them to be'. He was referring to the raw materials buyer, production planner, market forecaster and distribution manager. 'They are all affected by whatever each one does. If they can't work as a team, then I know only too well what will happen to our narrow profit margins'.

The same is true in every walk of life. Chartered accountant audit teams, on-site project groups, film crews, operating theatre teams, all require talented individual specialists who have acquired the desire and ability to work effectively together in teams.

This need becomes greater in the fast-changing world where the permanent teams at board or operational level or in the functional areas, such as management services, are complemented by numerous temporary task groups in matrix-type organisations. These can increase your flexible response to change; they can stimulate creativity, innovation and productivity within the organisation. These teams form, disperse and reform. How can such matrix organisations work as teams? How do you equip yourself with the necessary team building skills? Part Two is designed to help you to answer these questions.

It is relatively easy to establish a degree of teamwork or co-operation between a group of people; it is infinitely harder to develop a high-performance team. In Part Two we are concerned with identifying the factors that go into the making and sustaining of such teams.

To achieve excellence in results over a period of time in an organisation, as in a football team, is not accidental. The various properties of groups identified in Part One – communication, decision making, cohesiveness, morale, atmosphere, standards, procedures – are all found again in high-performance teams but to different degrees. The average work group and the exceptional team can be compared to two horses: both have the same muscles, legs, lungs and other organs. But one is an ordinary riding horse in the local stables, the other is a three times winner of the Grand National. Why is one different from the other?

In the transformations of a work group into a team, and an ordinary team into a high-performance team, attention must be given to three crucially important elements: leadership, membership and common methods or strategies of working together.

Teams need good leadership, but high-performance teams need very good leadership. What do we mean by good/very good in this context? What is this scale of merit? In *Effective Leadership* I introduced the distinction between leaders for good and 'good leaders'. Hitler, for example, was a 'good leader' in the sense that he could inspire people to follow him, but he was the archetypal misleader – leading people in the wrong direction. Here I shall assume that the leader's ends are good and concentrate on good leadership in the second sense, namely *having the appropriate skills to lead effectively*.

The same distinction, incidentally, applies to teams. Doubtless the teamwork of those responsible for exterminating millions of Jews in the Second World War in the concentration camps was of a very high order, but the ends towards which their co-operative efforts worked were wholly evil.

Personally, to continue the diversion for a moment, I do not believe these two meanings of the word good can ultimately be separated. My reasons for believing that can be detected in the concept of the person outlined in Chapter 5. If we are indeed basically moral as humans then we cannot give ourselves forever to immoral purposes. The structure of reality works against us, slowly perhaps but always inexorably. In the longer term the leader for bad (and the team for bad) will not survive.

In the high-performance team the personal qualities of the

leader complement his functional skills in the task and group areas. Not only will he provide direction and build the team, he (or she) will also add a subtle touch of inspiration.

The ability to inspire others is a general characteristic of good leaders. It is especially important if the group or organisation is working in difficult conditions or adverse circumstances, where morale can easily fall. Hitler could recognise this quality of leadership in others intuitively, doubtless because he possessed it so abundantly himself. In deciding to appoint Rommel to command the Afrika Korps in 1941 he said:

> I picked up Rommel because he knows how to *inspire* his troops. This is absolutely essential for the commander of a force that has to fight under particularly arduous climatic conditions like North Africa.

If we ask, 'Why did such-and-such a group or organisation, which was perfectly ordinary, become a high-performance team or an excellent organisation?', the answer is often that they were *inspired* to raise their sights and standards by the vision, enthusiasm and drive of a particular leader. Therefore it is impossible to divorce effective teambuilding from effective leadership.

The drawback of putting too much emphasis on the leader is that it seems to diminish the role of being a member. The normal counterpart of being a leader is being a follower. We are not ashamed to call ourselves followers of an outstanding leader (Jews, Christians and Moslems are all disciples or followers of Moses, Jesus and the Prophet Mohammed) but, in the context of industry, being a follower strikes some people as being not an appropriate image. Being a team member sounds much more positive.

Membership – this second ingredient in effective teamwork – is best approached through the concept of role. In Chapter 14 I shall review, and dismiss, much of the recent theorising about roles in groups. These have either concentrated upon trivial roles that people assume in groups, or are assigned by the group members, such as 'funny man', 'know all' or 'father figure', or they have personified particular functions (as we saw in the Benne-Sheats lists in Chapter 4).

We are left, then, with two positive roles open to colleagues in a group, those of leader and team member. We must reject the idea that leadership (in the sense of the provision of task, team and individual functions) is a cake, and the more share the leader has, the less cake there will be for the members. As one very good leader, the chief executive of an electronics engineering company, said to me, 'I have never had so much authority until I started giving it away'.

The idea that there is a team member role, complementary rather than antithetical to the leader's role, and equally positive, is a novel one. What is the content of it? In a high performance team, apart from the all-important specialist roles, the team members' general role consists of being the kind of person able to provide functions to achieve the task, build and maintain the team and develop or encourage other individuals. In a low-grade team a given individual may be good at one or two of these functions only, such as evaluating or summarising – hence the tendency to label them 'roles' and personify them. He will lack the range and flexibility of a really good team member.

For in a high productivity team the social competence of members is such that they can turn their hand to many functions. They are thoroughly flexible, not putting themselves or others into the strait-jackets of 'role' definitions.

In this respect leadership and membership so conceived are remarkably similar. But this should cause us no surprise. Moreover it is an asset, for managers are both leaders in one situation and team members (subordinates and colleagues) in others. Such an understanding should enable them to change hats without a crashing of gears, to mix metaphors.

Where leaders and team members differ in role is that the latter are more likely to continue special responsibilities – technical or professional – with their team membership role than are leaders. The roles of leader and member do not exist in a vacuum. They are always combined with other roles; the leader is also manager, doctor, head of department, commanding officer, bishop, and so on. The team member, following that order, may be computer specialist, anaesthetist, admissions tutor, signals officer or archdeacon. In the team context he will contribute more than the leader in his technical/professional role. There is a sense in which the role of leader is to ensure that everyone else in the team is effectively performing *their* roles.

For leaders and members to blend together to produce results of excellence in their field, a third element – common methods or strategies for doing things – is necessary. A football team needs its well-rehearsed drills. A first-rate musical concert is the product of a competent inspiring conductor, an orchestra of outstanding instrumentalists who are working together as a team, and, thirdly, a common score, such as Mozart's Symphony No. 21.

This analogy breaks down at a certain point, for the equivalent in industry to Mozart's score is the plan which the team itself formulates or implements. It is often composer or author, writing its own script, as well as actor. But it needs some sketchmap, some frame of reference, that will help it to interpret what it is doing and give it some method of diagnosing failure. A better comparison would be a science research laboratory, where the scientists and technicians engaged in different activities would all subscribe to scientific method, a system for testing and recording discovery which can be described and to some extent broken down into its constituent parts.

There is no one equivalent to the scientific method in teamwork generally. But I believe that a combination of the three circles model and a framework for decision making, problem solving and innovative thinking represents a minimum requirement. If not the musical score itself they represent the means of setting out the music.

These three elements – leader, member and shared processes – are the subjects of chapters in Part Two.

9 Teams

What is a team? What makes a *good* team? These are simple questions and we tend to think we know the answers – until someone asks!

The word 'team' is often used loosely, sometimes merely as a synonym for group. But there are no synonyms in the language. A team can be distinguished from a group. Or rather, in the words of Bernard Babington Smith[16], a team is

> a group in which the individuals have a common aim and in which the jobs and skills of each member fit in with those of others, as – to take a very mechanical and static analogy – in a jigsaw puzzle pieces fit together without distortion and together produce some overall pattern.

The two strands in this definition – a common task and complementary contributions – are essential to the concept of a team. An *effective* team may be defined as one that achieves its aim in the most efficient way and is then ready to take on more challenging tasks if so required.

THE COMMON AIM

The first questions a person – potential leader or member – should ask himself are: 'Is a team needed? Does this task require the complementary efforts of a group of people?' These raise the further questions: 'Why do teams arise in the first place? What are the kinds of task that need teamwork?'

Often the source of a team lies in one person doing a job that he discovers is too large for him in the time available. You can mow a large cricket field with a motor mower, but if you have an assistant to remove and empty the grassbox when full you can do the job in less time.

The example can be developed into others where two, three, four people and so on are needed. That involves the 'author' of the group, now most probably the leader, getting to know the members, their abilities and characteristics. Initially, when

Nature of task	*Implications*
Can be carried out by a single person, but time required is not available.	Several people doing the *same work* may complete the task in the given time, for example, 500 envelopes that need to be addressed, filled, stamped by and despatched in the afternoon post. Each knows what to do and does it independently.
Effort or force required cannot be exerted by one person, for example, to lift a lorry off someone who has been knocked down.	A group of people must work together. A degree of co-ordination will be needed between the operatives.
Several distinct operations are required at the same time or in concert for example an orchestra.	Here someone beyond the operators may be needed to organise and co-ordinate, for example a conductor.

Fig. 9.1 Working Together

they come together, he will be the central person. For he will know them all individually, and they him, but not each other: this fact alone puts him in the commanding position. If he is paying them, too, this position will be even stronger.

Bernard Babington Smith has suggested that the kinds of task that require teamwork – a concerted effort by a number of people – can be set out as shown in Fig. 9.1.

It is important, then, to check whether or not a particular task needs teamwork in the third sense of *complementary* effort. A class of schoolchildren working on arithmetic is a group of individuals, not a team. Of course if they tackle a history project, put on a play or play hockey they will have to work as members of a team. In the first case the working group is the *context* for individual work; in the other instances the group is an *instrument* for achievement.

In all these cases, however, the principle of co-operation or concerted effort pays off. As Homer wrote, 'Light is the task when many share the toil'. But not all match up to this definition of a team:

> Teams are groups of people who co-operate to carry out a joint task. They may be assigned to different work roles, or be allowed to sort them out between themselves and change jobs when they feel like it, for example the crews of ships and aircraft, research teams, maintenance gangs and groups of miners.[17]

EXPERTS AND TEAMS

Josephine Klein in *The Study of Groups* (1956)[18], devoted her first chapter to the performance of tasks in groups. She attempted to describe more precisely in what circumstances it will be worthwhile to form a group.

Let us assume, she postulated first, that the members of a group are equal in strength and skill, and the task they perform is very simple. If some men are pulling a rope as hard as they can, the addition of another man will increase the power of the group, but it decreases the average contribution made by the members. You do not calculate the total strength of the group by adding the individual 'strengths' of members. Each man's contribution is a marginal one.

Klein cited more research studies which indicate that

interaction between members may have an adverse effect on the total output of a number of persons. These disadvantages are only important, however, when the task is simple, the goal all-important to the members and the duration of the group so short that the problems of keeping members happy do not arise. Where these conditions are not present, interaction with others will support the positive aspects of the task or help to compensate for its negative deficiencies.

Klein concluded, therefore, that where the task is simple and the members equal in strength, the task will be done more effectively if there is no interaction between members, except in so far as they are organised by an 'entrepreneur' with whom they all interact and who works out the final solution.

Let us imagine, Klein suggests next, an *unequal* degree of skill among the members. Here some research studies support the conclusion that interaction between members of the group will enable the less-skilled members to solve the problems because of the help they receive from the presence of more-skilled or knowledgeable members. The expert present will develop a solution to benefit the whole group – provided of course that the problem is such that the expert solution can be recognised as correct. If it cannot be, then the group could spend a long time discussing the merits of different solutions.

The predicament of an expert in such a situation now becomes clearer. A group in such circumstances tends to distract an expert from his best performance. If he is right, but not obviously right as far as the others are concerned, he is held back while he attempts to persuade his colleagues. If he is obviously right, the group will accept his judgement, but then why, you may ask, was a group needed in the first place? Most probably because the expert's decisions need to be executed by others who will feel more involved and committed if they have participated in making the decision or solving the problem. 'The expert must therefore have skill in human relations as well as in his own field if he is to function usefully in a group where other members are less skilled than he is', concluded Klein.

In addition the expert working in a group does have the benefit of testing his own ideas out against those of the rest of the group, a useful insurance policy against him pursuing a line of thought longer than is useful. For the group's comments may make him go back and review the problem as a whole; even the questions of untrained members may rescue him from following a narrow and unfruitful tramline of an approach. Here a good leader can help by facilitating suggestions and the testing of ideas between the members in group discussion. Here are some guidelines for leaders of committees or discussion groups:

CHECKLIST

- Have you understood the question, problem or need for decision, assessed the available information, and asked members to give their opinions or make their contributions?

- Do you then identify the key issues? Do you try to reach agreement where opinions differ on these issues?

- In the light of the agreed objective or policy do you assess the value of the available contributions or proposals?

- Do you stimulate the committee to consider other options?

- Can you break down large problems into manageable pieces and deal with them systematically?

- Are you sure that the committee has genuinely weighed the pros and cons of the feasible alternatives?

- As custodian of the rules of procedure, do you interpret them firmly but flexibly?

Supposing, lastly, that a task is so complicated that more than one expert is needed to solve it. When it can be broken down into a number of smaller problems, which have to be worked out consecutively or in parallel, these can be tackled by several experts. You need in effect a series of little experts rather than one big one in such cases. Members can make three kinds of contribution: correct suggestions, correct criticisms or 'trigger' suggestions (incorrect in themselves but triggering off correct responses in others).

Clearly we are here over the threshold of teamwork. Each member is an expert in his own way. Each member has a special skill to contribute to the task and can also perform some useful functions – for example, making 'trigger' suggestions – unrelated to his expert field.

Both Babington Smith and Klein implicitly warn us against: (1) assuming that all tasks need teamwork – some are tackled best individually – and (2) that all work groups are teams. Committees, for example, are not the same as teams, although they also are task-oriented collections of individuals bound by a set of obvious rules.

Groups do not think or create new ideas in the way that individuals do. The individual members think and create; the group accepts, modifies or builds upon, or rejects that thinking. In that sense groups do make decisions; they may prompt and encourage but they do not create new ideas. As Tom Douglas concludes:

> The individual tends to operate much more effectively, not exactly in isolation, but more independently in all areas of human behaviour that can be called 'creative'. No one, to the best of my knowledge, ever created anything of value as a member of a group except those factors which pertain to the group, as for instance support or reflection and exchange of ideas. Thus no painter ever created a worthwhile painting as a group. Of course there are many examples of groups executing paintings – the students of some master, like Rubens, for instance – but the guiding genius and overseeing creative intelligence was that of the master and not the pupils. Likewise no book or piece of music, no drama, no truly creative work can be performed by a group except in similar circumstances, namely, under the overall direction of a creative individual.[19]

CHECKLIST

● What are the origins and nature of the common task?

● Does the task require teamwork?

● Is it too complex for any one individual to tackle successfully on his own?

● In order to succeed, is it essential that there should be more than one expert or specialist in the team?

● What are the specialist skills or knowledge necessary?

● Is there a leader who can blend together expert and inexpert contributions, such as 'trigger suggestions', at every stage of the team's work?

● Is the task a creative one, best tackled by gifted individuals with assistants, together with opportunity for regular discussion with colleagues?

● Would setting up a committee, rather than establishing a team, be more appropriate?

TEAMWORK ON THE SHOPFLOOR

So far I have emphasised the one-way influence of the task upon the nature of the group. But, to a more limited extent, the process works the other way. If you have people who work well together, with mutual trust and affection, they tend to introduce a degree of co-operation into their common work not strictly called for by the job itself. School children, for example, may help each other with their homework. Committees made up of those who know, respect and like each other will operate with a strong commitment to a common goal, making decisions in a quite different way from committees made up of individuals each representing vested interests.

The same principle applies throughout working life. It has been found that interaction between people on the shopfloor reinforces positive job satisfaction and helps to alleviate any unavoidable elements of toil, drudgery or unpleasant working conditions.

Routine machine work generally isolates the operative from everyone else. That does not happen if it is one of those rare machines which requires two or more people to operate it, as distinct from tending to parts of it. The operative is thus cut off from one of the more rewarding aspects of older technology – the necessity to blend one's working activities continuously with the activities of a partner or partners. The effects of the older technologies sometimes seem anomalous to the outsider: a group working together, with complementary activities, may develop a very high morale in spite of apparently dreary work and appalling conditions. The lesson was summed up in the perceptive comment of someone watching two team members at a tannery who spent hour after hour – together – heaving 70lb untreated hides on to a cutting table. They moved in unison, since they had to, and this elementary activity was the focus for a succession of energetic activities by a dozen other men. 'Look', was the comment, 'they're dancing'.

Two hefty hidesmen would have found the comment preposterous but when one looked at the much cleaner, less strenuous, but infinitely drearier machine activities elsewhere in the tannery, the lack of a 'dance' – any genuinely complementary activity by anyone else – was all too apparent.

In the past two decades there have been well-publicised attempts, notably in Sweden at the Volvo plants, to introduce teamwork into the routine work of the automobile assembly line. Some of these have been successful, some less so. Cultural background, previous experience and expectations of operatives, methods of pay and bonus or incentive, trade union attitudes and, above all, quality of leadership shown by managers and supervisors: these are the key factors in determining the success or failure of teamwork in manufacturing industry.

CASE STUDY:
THE END OF THE ASSEMBLY LINE?

Nissan make cars and lorries. It is the world's largest motor manufacturer. The Nissan factory at Smyrna in Tennessee is the largest Japanese investment in America. Under American management – there are only 15 Japanese in a work force of 1900 – it has been judged one of America's best run companies.

The work force is broken down into teams, each responsible for one part of production. There is no demarcation between jobs: each member is trained to do someone else's job. 'No one talks of my job', said one, 'we talk of *our* job'. In planning work schedules the teams rotate the dull jobs that cannot yet be taken over by robots. There is no demeaning clocking-in at 7.00 am. Each team gathers for ten minutes to discuss production, allocate tasks, solve problems and, if necessary, air grievances.

But the teamwork principle does not always work. General Motors found this out in the early 1970s. Despite successes in pilot schemes in plants to build some parts of vehicles in teams instead of on assembly lines, senior management eventually concluded that 'group experiments may suit some people but not all'. By 1975 they could cite several instances to support that conclusion.

'The GM assembly division has built Chevrolet vans for many years and this has become a fairly simplified product', noted one manager. They took four men and women to a separate building and tried to educate them to build a van. They had the assistance of an engineer who worked with them to get started. Building a van on the assembly line takes eight man hours per man. At first these people were taking thirteen to fourteen man hours. But eventually they got to the point where they could build the van in a little less than one and half hours per man. Finally we put that van assembly job in Detroit with another team alongside the ordinary moving assembly lines.

Some people on the team soon decided they preferred working on the assembly line and the department had to juggle its personnel until it had a group that liked team work. Adds a senior executive: 'We intended to put the team building approach through the whole plant. But when we surveyed the workers, they just didn't want it'.

In a typical assembly operation, the man has a fairly simple job assignment. He doesn't have a multiplicity of things to do. He can develop a style, a method and a rhythm which permit him to do the job in his own way and at his own pace.

In a group system the individual has a lot of things to do. The whole psychology of the job has been changed for him. He has a much greater responsibility than before and he finds it quite frustrating because instead of three elements to his operation he now has twenty or thirty. When he gets to number thirteen or fourteen he starts to think: 'Oh my God did I do number seven?' The people told us they didn't like this extra responsibility. . . . It is clear that GM sees only a limited future for team building, if only on practical grounds. . . . One of the biggest problems is supplying materials and parts. A car may contain upwards of 15 000 parts. 'How', asked a senior manager, 'could you possibly store that many parts where they would be accessible to five or ten men?

You can experiment with a group if it is a very simple vehicle and if the production volume is very low'.

Adds the Chairman of General Motors: 'I don't ever foresee the end of the assembly line. We may see different approaches to sub-assembly, to break down the job so that it can be done more effectively. But our experience in the plant is this: the greatest difficulty we have with our employees is not because the job is repetitive so much as the fact we have to change the job, which we frequently have to do because of product development or new investment'.[20]

Perhaps the most significant innovation in recent years has been the introduction of Quality Circles into factories and offices. This practice, pioneered in America, adopted by Japan in a big way, and thence taken up in Europe, is a simple one. It encourages leaders to get their groups together to identify and solve problems, critically review work practices and search creatively for incremental innovations, all to the end of improving product quality and customer service.

SEQUENTIAL TEAMS

Question: When is a team not a team?
Answer: When it is apart.

Do you agree?

So far we have considered teams as face-to-face groups working together on a project. But there are many teams where members may be working out of sight or earshot from each other for much of the time. Teamwork still continues in these conditions, at least in high-performance teams.

Here work is not done obviously in concert together, like an orchestra playing a symphony. All have to work in a particular sequence: for example, the plasterer cannot do his work until the bricklayer has finished building the walls; the tiler cannot do his work until the joiner has finished the roof. How good the finished house is depends upon each doing his job properly. If only one of them does not succeed in doing this, the whole project is ruined. Remember that the major cost of the house is the cost of the labour and this is important because the final price of the house depends upon each person doing his work effectively and using his time efficiently.

Viewed in this sequential way almost everyone who works on their own is really part of a team. An enterprising schoolteacher used the example of the building industry to

---

Teaching teamwork in school

This report by a school teacher illustrates how a realistic and broad concept of teamwork can be taught in the classroom:

In this phase we looked at jigsaws with pieces missing and saw how this can spoil the whole picture. We talked about various mechanical instruments and how they are useless if only one small part is missing or does not work. I encouraged the children to draw pictures of anything they liked, with one part missing and the others then tried to spot what was wrong with it and what effect this would have.

This then led into a discussion on teams and how each member of a team depends upon each other. The children tended to think of sports teams that they are part of at school. I tried to lead them to think of other teams especially ones found in certain work situations.

I invited certain people to come and talk to them about their work and their role as part of a team:

1   A postman explained the people involved in delivering any letter posted in one of our local post boxes

2 A telephone engineer explained the people involved in installing a phone, the cables, the exchange and the maintenance of these

3 A teacher explained how the staff of a school could be considered to be part of a team

4 A worker in a local biscuit factory explained all the people involved to produce a packet of biscuits

In all cases I asked the speaker to stress the importance of every person involved in 'their team' and how the final aim could not be achieved if any one member of the team was missing or did not do what was expected of them'.

introduce a programme on teamwork in industry. The second phase was called 'Missing parts and missing people'.

The way to judge the effectiveness of 'sequential teams' is to look at their performance from the standpoint of the customer or client. For that is the only person who *experiences* the result – or lack of result – of the whole team. If one member, one link in the chain, is weak that will cancel out the effects of the other members. The well-designed train may get you there safely and on time; the guard and ticket collector may be courteous; designer, manufacturer, driver, guard and ticket-collector, as well as time-tabler, booking clerk, station manager, have all done their parts well; but if the cleaners have not bothered, and the train is filthy, the customer may well go away with that damaging image in his mind. Next time he may choose to travel by air or coach.

The all-star team

Too many cooks spoil the broth. A chain is no stronger than its weakest link. Platitude upon platitude, but relevant.

The sequential procedure is like a multi-stage rocket where any part can fail, and the failure rate of each component determines the failure rate of the whole project.

Let us suppose we have a five-stage rocket on the launching pad. Assume 90 per cent reliability for each stage. The resultant reliability of the rocket is 90 per cent of 90 per cent of 90 per cent of 90 per cent of 90 per cent – or 59 per cent. In a five-stage rocket with 80 per cent dependability at each stage, the chance of success is only 33 per cent. Forget it.

Where successive stages in a process are interdependent, quality of performance at each phase is crucial. Putting more men on the job is not necessarily going to help – the quality has to be right. What you need is an all-star team.

Alan Simpson in *The Financial Post*, Canada

Who is leading (motivating, inspiring) in a dispersed or sequential team? The manager cannot be everywhere at the same time.

In a sense leadership has to be built into each individual member – he has to be a self-leader. That means not just being a self-starter in terms of motivation and work but also someone who can sustain himself. He has also 'internalised' – both the standards of his profession and the team's standards. When there is no one around to chivvy, chase or cajole, these are the standards he will stick to. –

There is an analogy here with an artist, who works alone but exemplifies one meaning of integrity: adherence to artistic standards outside himself. If the picture does not come up to scratch or the poem fails to evolve or the music is below par, the true artist throws it away. He does not need anyone else to evaluate his performance; he knows when he has done a good job.

The analogy can be taken a step further. For the author – apparently practitioner of a solitary craft – can be seen as a member of a dispersed team; some of the members – editor, indexer, book designer, picture researcher, copy editor – he may meet, and others – printer, salesmen, warehouse manager, bookseller – he probably never will.

It is quite possible, and probably very desirable, to develop in ourselves and in others this sense of being members of a team apart – or rather many teams apart. It saves the self-employed and the individual contributor in organisations from the barren rocks of individualism.

CORE PURPOSE AND AIMS

Leadership includes the notion of direction. It follows that self-leaders (members of dispersed teams) have a sense of direction. They will share a knowledge and commitment to the common task, despite being out of face-to-face interaction or even when removed from regular contact by telephone or letter. Moreover, they will have sufficient trust and confidence in their unseen leader and colleagues to know that they also are pressing ahead on agreed lines and according to accepted standards.

In this context it is not enough to know just the objectives. When people are out of contact with their manager and a problem or obstacle crops up that makes it impossible to attain objectives or compels a major deviation from the plan, what do they do?

To exercise their initiative in the proper way each member of a dispersed team must be clear about its core purpose. The core purpose is the answer to the question:

Why does the group exist at all?

or

What is the special and specific contribution it makes to some wider system? (that is, the business or organisation as a whole)

This is different from defining its objectives or goals at a particular point.

Of course knowledge of its core purpose is really essential for all teams. For this will serve as a navigation mark for thinking about goals, structure, priority of activities, and allocation of resources. Many of the ailments in these areas can be traced back to a lack of clarity and agreement about the primary purpose of the organisation.

Ideally it should be possible to describe the core purpose succinctly in one sentence. Not that any one wording should be regarded as sacrosanct; indeed that short definition of purpose should frequently be rephrased to keep it fresh and alive.

Aims are middle term – the bridges which span the river between core purpose and the more concrete, tangible, specific objectives and priorities of the next short-term. Knowing the relevant aim means that you can be flexible: if one route (objective, plan) to the goal is blocked you can still press on towards a state defined as an aim. You can take alternative routes. If you do not know the aim, the eclipse of an objective will leave you in the dark. You have no alternative but to ask or wait for new orders.

POINTS TO PONDER

A team is essentially a group with a common aim in which the technical skills and personal abilities of the members are complementary. A high achieving team has all the properties of a more ordinary team but in an enhanced degree.

Each member is both an expert and skilled team member in performing functions needed by the task, maintenance and other individuals.

Teams often grow from one person who is their author and leader. If so, such a person needs to shift the centre from himself to the co-operative efforts of the team.

The test of a good team is whether or not its members can work as a team while they are apart, contributing to a sequence of activities rather than to a common task which requires their presence in one place and at one time.

A core purpose produces real commitment

CASE STUDY:
TEAMWORK IN THE CONSTRUCTION INDUSTRY

John Armitt, Deputy Managing Director of John Laing International Limited, addressed a British Institute of Management conference on the theme of 'Creating Commitment in Project Based Industries' in 1985. He painted a picture of declining orders for the industry and the vital importance – once work had been won against fierce competition – for outstanding on-site performance. How is this achieved? He continued:

Taylor Woodrow has as its logo men pulling on a rope. We in Laing have a house magazine called 'Team Spirit' and teamwork is an often used phrase in construction. No one man can conceptualise, design, construct and commission a project. It requires the efforts and skills of many people and the successful projects occur when individual skills are brought together at the right time with the individuals having a personal desire to succeed with what they are doing and having a commitment to the achievement of the common goal.

For the individual, then, the commitment means the seeking of personal success. Within the team commitment means 'are you with us? Is your objective the same as ours?'. So when we say that Bill is very committed, we are saying he works hard, he does not allow obstacles to deter him, he will accept views other than his own in order to achieve the end result and he strives to ensure the achievement of his goal. The answer as to how do we get Bill to do these things must lie in providing answers to the question, 'Why does Bill act in this way?' I have already mentioned the negative incentive: fear of unemployment – and certainly absenteeism has dropped in the last five years.

On the positive side there is of course financial reward, or economic necessity. The traditional view, particularly in our industry, is that the chance to receive more money will cause people to work harder and by being committed to their own personal desires, the group goal is also achieved.

Anyone who worked on the Isle of Grain power station will know a lot of men earned very good money, but the project was not a success. It was late, it cost more than anyone expected and only for a very few of these men did their commitment go beyond maximising their pay. CEGB had a goal to build Europe's largest oil-fired power station economically and on time. The directors of the various contractors involved had the same goal but neither succeeded in getting the 2000 men working on the projects to share or meet that goal. Monetary reward was not enough and the achieving of a personal goal did not mean that the common goal was also achieved. As managers, therefore, we must try to combine these personal and common goals.

In John Laing we are primarily concerned with the construction stages of a project and so I will work through that looking at personal and common goals.

Estimators have a single goal to win work. Most of the time this is achieved by submitting the lowest price. However, it must also be a price for which others in the team can actually build the job. Each tender probably lasts upon average no more than six weeks and what is required is initiative, determination and acceptance of the deadline imposed by the tender closing date. On average they probably only succeed one in ten times. How does a man maintain commitment to a task which has a limited success rate?

When the contract is won the construction team under the project manager have to build the job for the money allowed in the tender. What will cause them to try to do so?

For a client the project must be finished on time and within his budget. How does he get the construction team to share his goals?

I believe the answer to all these questions is in fact very similar.

First, I would like to make an analogy. In a football match the players know quite clearly the timescale, the boundaries of the pitch, what their manager expects of them as individuals, (that is, their role in the team) and there is an overriding objective, which is to put the ball into the opponent's net. Football managers work with their players all the time, both in training and during the match. Just because the centre forward knows how to kick the ball and what he is meant to do, he is not just left from one week to another to get on with it. He is cajoled, trained, encouraged, taught new tricks, concern is shown for his health and a clear identity and pride in his team encouraged and developed. The main form of communication is verbal. It may not always be very polite, particularly from the fans who are his 'client'. In our business we must do the same. Projects are like a game of football. We have a fixed period, we have a specification and, within each element of the project, we can identify single goals.

The fixed period is a particular advantage in our business. Just as at the end of ninety minutes the football manager can review performance, learn from the mistakes and go out for a fresh start the following Saturday, so we have the same opportunities between projects. Our people are also used to moving around. So just as a football manager makes substitutions, we can change our project team during the project if we do not have the correct mix of people. Our project's success is a matter of ensuring that at each stage the individuals involved can relate to what is required and understand their part.

The tender is in many ways the easiest, but often the most ignored. I believe the successful tenders are those that are consciously managed. All those involved: estimators, engineers, buyers, quantity surveyors, planners, and so on must be brought together at regular intervals. People should not be left in their departmental box to do their particular thing in a vacuum. At the beginning of the tender basic strategies must be agreed. For example, how much are we going to sublet? Are there any new sources of labour or materials to be considered this time? Will there be any advantage in trying to produce a different programme from

the one that the client is looking for? Thereafter regular
follow-up meetings must be held to review progress and the
final settlement must not be rushed. A clear indication of
how committed the contract's director is to winning the job
will be shown by how much time he makes available for the
settlement meeting.

When the Laing Molam ARC joint venture won the
Falklands Airfield project I was not that surprised. At the
outset the joint venture Board appointed a single bid
manager. There were very extensive discussions and a free
exchange of experience on labour, plant and staffing levels
and material resources. Each company then concentrated
upon particular aspects of the project and every week the
team was brought together and the progress reviewed. On
the day of the submission, the tender team worked until
2.30 am looking for a rather large sum of money which had
disappeared in the computer. Two days were given to the
actual settlement meeting, with the Chairmen and Senior
Directors of all the companies in attendance. Nobody
doubted anyone's commitment to winning the project and
that can be very infectious.

On site the project manager has the responsibility of
winning commitment. To do this he must set clear goals
and targets which can be achieved. He must be seen to be
making decisions and he must lead by example. He must
have as much concern for the quality of the food as the
quality of the concrete. I believe the project manager is the
absolute keystone to the success of any project. He must be
prepared to lead and recognise that all his decisions are not
going to be popular.

The project manager who commands respect will also be
a long way towards obtaining commitment. His role is very
much one of a communicator and here I would like to
emphasise my preference for verbal as opposed to written
communication. Written communication takes time and
often is used to say things which the writer has not the
courage to say and it generates in the recipient the belief
that he must also put pen to paper and reply.

How does the project manager obtain the commitment of
the labour force, particularly at a time when it is difficult to
offer the prospect of continuous employment? I have twice
been involved with a large UK labour force working

overseas: in the late 1970s in Poland and more recently in the Falklands. In neither case have we operated an incentive scheme and in both cases we paid considerable attention to explaining what the project entailed, the why's and the wherefore's at the recruitment stage and I am quite sure that this paid dividends in the early days. What is equally important has been to repeat that exercise as the project progresses.

In Iraq we have had a major project consisting of several motorway interchanges with a large TCN workforce. As with any large project it is very difficult to visualise the end result. One of our draughtsmen produced a coloured perspective of one of the interchanges for a Chairman's site visit, it was so good that he was then asked to do one for each interchange and these were displayed around the site and in the canteen. This might seem a fairly simple thing, but it generated a lot of interest amongst the labour force, who could actually see what it was they were meant to be building and could see the intended result of their labour when they were working down a hole and filling it up with concrete.

We should not underestimate the benefit of the fact that we are in a creative industry. We once showed some managers of Pilkingtons around one of our projects. Afterwards, one of them said how he envied us. They spent their time trying to perfect something so that people would not see it! We have a permanent and very visible end result for our efforts. Models, artistic impressions, progress photographs, more often than not gather dust in the project manager's office. They are without doubt of interest to everybody who is involved in the project. Sites were opened on a Sunday to allow the men who were actually involved in building the job to bring their families and show them what they actually did for the other six days in the week. Whenever I have done that, it has undoubtedly been a great success. Most men are actually proud of what it is they are building.

On site men must be able to identify themselves with a particular group, to know their foreman, to be able to get on with their personal task and to be fairly paid. This may all seem fairly obvious, but the one I would particularly like to emphasise is that of enabling people to get on with their task. In my experience if men have the tools, the materials and continuity of operation, then they will set-to with a purpose. Time and time again disputes and poor productivity arise because as managers we do not ensure that those parameters are met. Going back to the football match, you would not expect the centre forward to give of his best on a wet pitch if his boots had no studs. . . .

How do we increase the commitment of our staff to our company as a whole? Again we must look for a combination of personal and corporate or team objectives. As managers of a company we must try and ensure that we know the personal ambitions of our staff and in Laing we do this by annual formal reviews in a one-to-one discussion, from which flow training programmes and the setting and monitoring of objectives. Staff rotation is I believe of particular interest and benefit in the international business. By this I mean site personnel also doing Head Office support jobs, hopefully realising that for support teams to be effective they need maximum co-operation and information from the site.

Also by switching your UK support team at regular intervals, you can generate a project-type attitude in the Head Office. This will always generate more commitment than just being part of the Head Office mass. Clearly we must ensure that pay and conditions are competitive and pension schemes will provide longer term security.

Company objectives will again mean staff mobility in which case the company must be aware of the domestic problems that this will cause and be sympathetic and helpful in its policies.

If a company can demonstrate by its action that *it* has commitment to its staff, then the staff are more likely to return that commitment.

In Laing in the last few years we have developed on a regular basis quite large staff meetings. All the staff in a region will gather together and the local director will explain what the business is doing, how it is doing, what the problems are, how he sees the future and what the actual financial results have been. Then the floor is open for general questions and discussion. Subsequent surveys have shown that staff actually enjoy these sessions, feel they are worthwhile and would like more. It is a move towards more open management and actually treats employees as being responsible and sensible. We should not be surprised if the end result of that is that the staff return the compliment.

How does the company provide a picture of itself which causes people to be able to say with pride that they work with so-and-so? This will always be as a result of good management which ensures that quality work is always expected and that a caring face is shown to a local community. The basic honesty in business is seen as a guiding principle and that simple things like the company plant is kept clean and that people actually care that it is seen on the roads and the streets in its proper colours. In general it is seen that the company cares about its public image. All of this will be dependent upon the leadership and standards set from the very top of any organisation.

At the end of the day, however, I still believe that people primarily relate to other individuals. Attitude surveys within Laing have shown time and time again that job satisfaction is totally correlated to the satisfaction that they have with their immediate superior. Their loyalty first and foremost is going to be to their boss and he represents the company. If they know where they stand, know what is expected of them, see that as being fair and reasonable and feel that in difficulty they will have his support and commitment, then they will give commitment to him and in turn to the team and the company.

10 The leader

Preview of Chapter Ten

- What leadership is, and what it is not
- The fruits of leadership
- Your potential for leadership
- The keys to leadership
- Points to ponder

The importance of the leader in teamwork, teambuilding and team maintenance is clearly illustrated by the last case study. It stands out equally clearly from the literature about groups at work and about organisations as a whole. So much depends upon the quality of the leader – upon *your* leadership.

That raises several questions. First, what *is* leadership? Can you become more specific about it as a prelude to devising a programme for self-improvement. Secondly, how does leadership relate to team membership? Are all members who contribute functions really leaders? And, lastly, is leadership innate or can it be developed?

To discuss team building without an exploration in depth of the team leader – his personality and character, knowledge and experience, abilities and skills – strikes me as a pointless exercise. Orchestras may contain excellent violinists and woodwind players, there may be a marvellous composition in front of them, but if the conductor is not a leader they will not produce great music. Leadership – great leadership – is the theme of this chapter.

WHAT LEADERSHIP IS, AND WHAT IT IS NOT

Many of us tend still to believe that 'a leader' implies one person dominating another or a group of people. Research studies suggest that domineering individuals are not chosen or accepted leaders by others, except in situations such as prison. Physical strength or size, a dominant personality, or a will for power over others, is not the answer.

In industry, as in every other sphere where free and able people need to co-operate, effective leadership is founded upon respect and trust, not fear and submission. Respect and trust help to inspire whole-hearted commitment in a team; fear and submission merely produce compliance.

Leadership involves focusing the efforts of a group of people towards a common goal and enabling them to work together as a team. A leader should be directive in a democratic way.

For a leader is not there simply to co-ordinate functions. He helps the movement forwards in a given direction, through the efforts of individuals which complement and enhance each other. He recalls the group to the strengthening unity of a common purpose. A leader makes the parts whole.

Gang Leader

The musical *West Side Story* is the only introduction most of us have to the world of the street gang in America. In 1927 William F. Whyte wrote a book called *Street Corner Society* about the role of the gang in the life of underprivileged boys in Boston's Italian community and in particular a gang called the Nortons led by Doc. Members formed a well understood and fairly stable hierarchy: not only did the group usually do what the leader suggested, but each member's behaviour reflected his position in the power structure. Whyte decided that remarks travelled up the hierarchy during planning of group activities, and, when a decision had been reached at the top, flowed down to the lower ranks. It was not just a case of leaders telling followers what to do but a far more complex interaction between individuals in adjacent ranks. Whyte described the role of leader as follows:

The leader spends more money on his followers than they on him. The farther down the structure one looks, the fewer are the financial relations which tend to obligate the leader to a follower. . . The leader refrains from putting himself under obligations to those with low status in the group.

The leader is the focal point for the organisation of his group. In his absence, the members of the gang are divided into a number of small groups. There is no common activity or general conversation.

> When the leader appears . . . (he) becomes the central point in the discussion. A follower starts to say something, pauses when he notices that the leader is not listening, and begins again when he has the leader's attention. .
>
> The leader is the man who acts when the situation requires action. He is more resourceful than his followers. Past events have shown that his ideas are right. In this sense 'right' simply means satisfactory to the members. He is the most independent in judgement. . .
>
> When he gives his word to one of his boys, he keeps it. The followers look to him for advice and encouragement, and he receives more of their confidences than any other man. Consequently, he knows more about what is going on in the group than anyone else. . .
>
> The leader is respected for his fair-mindedness. Whereas there may be hard feelings among some of the followers, the leader cannot bear a grudge against any man in the group. He has close friends (men who stand next to him in position), and he is indifferent to some of the members; but if he is to retain his reputation for impartiality, he cannot allow personal animus to override his judgement. . .
>
> The leader does not deal with his followers as an undifferentiated group . . . (He) mobilises the group by dealing first with his lieutenant. . .
>
> The leadership is changed not through an uprising of the bottom men but by a shift in the relations between men at the top of the structure. When a gang breaks into two parts, the explanation is to be found in a conflict between the leader and one of his former lieutenants.
>
> William F. Whyte, *Street Corner Society*, University of Chicago Press, 1927

THE FRUITS OF LEADERSHIP

One of the chief fruits of good leadership is a good team. That principle seems universal in human society, and relevant, too, to the creatures who serve man. Studies of dog teams, for example, show that Siberian huskies can reach and sustain a speed of about 20 mph provided they have a good lead dog. That is a parable, if you like, for human teams.

The characteristics of the leader and the outcomes are related. They can be tabled as follows:

Characteristics	*Outcomes*
• Enthuser	• People are purposefully busy and everyone has a basis on which to judge priorities.

- Lives his values, such as integrity

- Sense of excitement. People willing to take risks. People willing to take on high work loads. Feelings of achievement.

- Leads by example

- Consistency. Followers know leader's values.

- Generates good leaders from his followers

- Is trusted by his followers.

- Aware of his own behaviour and of his environment

- People aspire to leader's example.

- Intellect to meet needs of his job

- Aware of the needs of the group he is leading and the needs of individuals

- The led start to lead. Leader becomes less indispensable. People are delegated to, coached and supported.

- Exhibits trust in his followers

- Able to represent the organisation to his people and his people to the organisation

- Followers feel they have some contribution to aims and are committed to them.

CASE STUDY: DEFINING THE MANAGER-LEADER

Imperial Chemical Industries made a profit of one billion pounds in 1985, the first British manufacturing company to do so. Five years previously one of their nine divisions was losing £100 million a year and two others were also in the red. The company put the development of management *leadership* as top of their personnel priorities. For ICI believed that if leadership is effective, people will:

- Have a clear sense of direction and work hard and effectively.

- Have confidence in their ability to achieve specific challenging objectives.

- Believe in and be identified with the organisation.

- Hold together when the going is rough.

- Have respect for and trust in managers.

- Adapt to the changing world.

ICI's divisions mounted a number of management development courses which put emphasis on what the manager *does* in order to achieve the task, build the team and develop individuals. How the leader does the necessary functions – style – is less important and varies from individual to individual. The management leader must:

- Feel personally responsible for his resources – human, financial and material. (Feeling and caring: a sense of responsibility.)

- Be active in setting direction and accepting the risks of leadership (being out in front).

- Be able to articulate direction and objectives clearly and keep his people in the picture.

- Use the most appropriate behaviour and methods to gain commitment to achievement of specific objectives (leaders don't stick to one style).

- Maintain high standards of personal performance and demand high standards of performance from others.

YOUR POTENTIAL FOR LEADERSHIP

Yes, there are such people as natural leaders. But they are an extremely rare breed. Most leaders, and indeed some of the most successful ones, are born *and* made. By that I mean they are endowed with a naturally high potential for leadership which they have discovered and set about consciously developing. They look upon leadership partly as an ability or skill which you can learn, practise and perfect.

Nor are leaders a 'type'. There is no one style of leadership that must be donned like a straitjacket on your personality.

'Leadership is being just *you*', said Lord Slim succinctly. You do not have to be an extrovert or aggressively cheerful. Successful leaders are very different. They all have strengths, personality and character, but these vary from individual to individual.

Consequently, an important aspect of leadership is knowing yourself. Knowing your own strengths and weaknesses is a key step on the path of making the most of what you have to offer. It is no good pretending to be someone you aren't: sooner or later your mask will slip. Any form of hypocrisy is anathema to a good leader. That does not mean, of course, that the leader will never act a part. He may have to act outwardly confident and calm, visibly stalwart and brave, when inwardly his feelings fall far short of these states. But here he is acting his best self, the person he truly is on his best days, not someone totally different from himself.

In the context of teambuilding, knowing your own strengths and weaknesses will ensure that you compensate for what you lack. It is fatal to select people to work with you who are clones of yourself. You should deliberately choose individuals who have strengths, knowledge and experience which you do not possess in considerable measure. Humility in this sense is a leadership asset.

THE KEYS TO LEADERSHIP

'To be a leader means to have determination', wrote Lech Walesa. 'It means to be resolute inside and outside, with ourselves and with others'.

The first responsibility of leadership is to define the objective. Achieving the aim is the ultimate test of leadership. Until you know clearly what it is you want to achieve you can't begin to direct other people towards it. When the objective or task is not easy to define the effective leader takes the time to think it out. Without a clear goal there is no such thing as concerted team work. Besides, who will follow a leader who does not know where he is going? 'If a blind man leads a blind man they will both fall into a ditch.'

Once the group's task is settled and the team have accepted, it is the individual's turn. He also needs a clear personal objective/or target. Naturally it must contribute to the overall aim, but the individual must see that it suits his strengths and skills. If possible it should be worked out with the individual concerned, so that he feels it his personal goal. Good targets should be:

- measurable
- time bounded
- realistic
- challenging
- agreed

Make sure each individual knows and feels that his part of the task is making a significant contribution to the group's overall task.

These elements – task, team and individual – constitute the core responsibility of the leader. They spring from the three overlapping areas of work group life already described in Chapter 6 and depicted there as a three circles, as in Fig. 10.1 below.

Fig. 10.1   The Leader's Core Responsibility

To fulfil the three circles of responsibility certain key functions have to be performed. They are the responsibility of the leader, but that does not mean the leader will do them all himself. They can be shared or delegated in all sorts of ways.

The following list is by no means definitive – the sheer variety of situations prohibit that – but these general functions are commonly required:

Planning	Seeking all available information; defining group task, purpose or goal; making a workable plan (in right decision-making framework)
Initiating	Briefing group on aims and plan; explaining *why* aim or plan is necessary; allocating tasks to group members; setting group standards
Controlling	Maintaining group standards; influencing tempo; ensuring all actions are taken towards objectives; keeping discussion relevant; prodding group to action/decision
Supporting	Expressing acceptance of persons and their contributions; encouraging group/individuals; disciplining group/individuals; creating team spirit; relieving tension with humour; reconciling disagreements or getting others to explore them
Informing	Clarifying task and plan; giving new information to the group, that is, keeping them 'in the picture'; receiving information from the group; summarising suggestions and ideas clearly
Evaluating	Checking feasibility of an idea; testing the consequences of a proposed solution; evaluating group performance; helping the group to evaluate its own performance against standards

It must be stressed again that not all these functions will be performed by every leader all the time. In groups of more than three or four there are too many actions required to meet the requirements of task, team and individual for any one person to do them. But the leader is *accountable* for the three circles. Taken together these functions constitute his role. Although team members may characteristically perform one or other of them – or contribute to several – the leader makes sure that they do so. He may have to do each of them himself as occasion requires. His range of functions will always be wider than any other single member.

Remember that you can be appointed a manager but you are not a leader until your appointment is ratified in the hearts and minds of those who work for you.

To deal effectively with people you must take time to understand them as persons. They need to be understood both in terms of what they share in common and what differentiates them. How does this particular person differ from all others? You do not have the *right* to know someone but you have the duty to try to do so. That does not mean being matey or familiar. It just means a willingness to spend time talking and listening. Effective leaders get about and meet people.

Give people your respect and trust, some real responsibilities together with a degree of independence and they will reward you with their best.

Lessons From History

'The best of men are but men at their best'

Major General John Lambert,
one of Cromwell's lieutenants

'I saw that he that will be loved, must love; and he that rather chooses to be more feared than loved, must expect to be hated, or loved but diminutively. And he that will have children, must be a father; and he that will be a tyrant must be content with slaves'.

Richard Baxter, on bishops who
persecuted the nonconformists

'Not geniuses, but average men require profound stimulation, incentive towards creative effort, and the nurture of great hopes'.

John Collier

'I am larger, better than I thought. I did not know I held so much'.

Walt Whitman

By contrast, if you treat people as things or numbers, they will respond without a spark of enthusiasm or an ounce of initiative. They will lack conviction and commitment. They will never discover through you that 'I am larger, better than I thought'.

Common sense should guide you in the matter of praise and criticism. Both are essential at the right time and in the right place. Judicious praise and recognition of a job well done mean a great deal to someone who takes pride in their work. It is no substitute for money or financial incentive, for praise does not fill an empty stomach. But it meets a very human need. And criticism, given firmly and tactfully in a positive, constructive way not only improves standards but also strengthens the bond of mutual respect. It shows that you care too much for the job – and ultimately for the team and the individual – to turn a blind eye to mistakes.

The proverbial wisdom of the nations has a wealth of advice – some of it contradictory – for leaders on this subject of praise and blame. Situations and the individual personalities of those concerned must guide you on which proverb to follow but the range of proverbs is thought-provoking. They reveal to us just how important giving and receiving praise is within the fabric of social life – someone once said to me that praise was the oxygen of the human spirit. But it is difficult both to give and receive it well.

Praise and Blame: Some Proverbs

An honest man is hurt by praise unjustly bestowed
Too much praise is a burden
I praise loudly, I blame softly
Our praise are our wages
The most pleasing of all sounds – that of your own praise
Be sparing in praise and more so in blaming
Praise a fool and you water his folly
Praise is always pleasant
Praise makes good men better and bad men worse

Finally, goodness in the moral sense is the sure foundation of leadership. Honesty, integrity, moral courage, justice or fairness, all make for better, more effective teams. Virtues such as these in leader and member alike mean that the energies of the team are being spent on the task, not on infighting, politicking, back-stabbing, intriguing and mutual suspicion. As with most things, it is up to you as leader to set the example.

POINTS TO PONDER

The principles of leadership sound simple and obvious. Not that your job as leader will ever be simple or easy. But the three circles model will serve you as a good guide through a maze of problems and personalities towards the common goal.

Good leadership makes everybody's work more effective and therefore more rewarding. That is *your* reward.

You will make demands on the team and on individual members; that is what you are there for as a leader. But you should always make more demands on yourself. 'To my fellow men, a heart of love; to myself, a heart of steel', as St Augustine said.

Team work is no accident, it is the by-product of good leadership

11 Teambuilding

All leaders are teambuilders. For teams are always either improving or declining in effectiveness. Therefore the work of teambuilding is never done.

More specifically, teambuilding applies when you are building a team in the first place or amalgamating two teams or organisations to form a new entity, or completely reconstituting and revitalising an old team.

Comparatively few leaders have the luxury of building their own teams in this second sense. Usually they inherit a team from somone else. The latter kind of team may include individuals who are 'brown at the edges', those who would not be there if you could start again and choose your own people. But you can make your own team. How do you go about it? How do you transform an assembly of individuals into a team?

That challenge may not be on your agenda now. But you never know when you might be asked to recruit and train a team for a particular task. It is bound to happen at least once – perhaps many times – in your career as a manager. Are you ready for it?

In this chapter I assume you are the leader and can select or build your own team. But the higher up the corporate ladder you climb the more you will be involved in building teams where you are not a member. The key appointment, of course, is then the leader. It is useful to remember when making it that the team leader has very distinctive responsibilities which more-or-less define the role:

- May be responsible for selection; if not, ought to be involved in it.

- Is responsible for ensuring that the standards and discipline of the team are such that high performance through interdependence happens.

- Allocates special responsibilities and controls the use of resources.

- Directs the formation of team strategy and plans.

- Has more to do with the team's interface with other groups and individuals involved in its performance.

- Will have to make considerable demands on the team as a group and on individual members.

SELECTING THE TEAM MEMBERS

As any good cook will tell you the excellence of a meal is largely determined by the quality of the ingredients that go into it. The importance of choosing the right people as team members from the collection of possible members can hardly be over-emphasised. It is the first principle of team success.

There are degrees of choice. It is rare that a manager is given permission – and an open cheque book – to go out into the world and choose whoever he pleases for his team. There are constraints on the pool of people from whom his choice must be made, as well as constraints of time under which he has to operate.

Occasionally, if there is genuinely a missing piece in the jigsaw puzzle, the leader can look beyond his part of the organisation or even outside the organisation itself. But compromises will almost certainly have to be accepted. You cannot be over-fastidious. Few good leaders have quite the team they would wish for – just as few good teams have quite the leader they would desire.

Shelves of books have been written on the subject of interviewing and choosing people for jobs. With the requirements of high performance teamwork in mind, their contents can be simplified into the three key factors:

- Technical or professional competence
- Ability to work as a team member
- Desirable personal attributes

Of course it helps if you already know the people well. Sometimes the larger group from which selections or substitutions must be made is just a list of names; at other times this supply group can be a very familiar reserve – like the reserves of a professional football team – clearly involved with the current team and often considered to be not only a reservoir but also a training group – in effect, already a part of the team.

The process can be compared to a funnel; wide at the top and narrowing down to the business end. The leader or selector starts with a fairly large number of people and eliminates potential members by a process of interviewing and testing.

Technical or professional competence

What is this person going to bring to the team? The first and most pressing requirement is that he or she should possess the skill or knowledge that is needed in the team. If your team requires a marketing specialist, for example, is this person merely a capable one or is he likely to make an outstanding contribution in the field of marketing.

As a leader you are most probably a generalist yourself. It may therefore be difficult for you to gauge the degree of professional ability of the person before you. Arguably, if you are aspiring to lead in that field, you should have *some* knowledge for making a judgement. The modern heresy that a management science exists that can be transferred from one industry to another has bred shallow managers, those who cannot assess the competences of those who work for them. Compare that with Napoleon who once declared:

There is nothing in the military profession that I cannot do for myself. If there is no one to make gunpowder, I know how to make it; gun carriages, I know how to construct them; if it is founding a cannon, I know that. If the details in tactics must be taught, I can teach them.

Nowadays, of course, not even a military general could say the same. A leader in any field should still have sufficient knowledge to be able to assess the professional worth of the members of his team but may have to associate specialists with him to make a judgement. The conductor of a first-class orchestra will have a general knowledge of instruments. He may play some of them himself and he will be a musician, able to detect that quality in others. But when it comes to selecting a new clarinet player for the orchestra he may well involve other woodwind specialists, either from within the orchestra or outside it.

Given that two candidates are equal in specialist competence (and as desirable team members) preference might well be given to the person who has a 'second string to his bow'. Many people have some other professional experience or technical expertise which is secondary to their main interest but could be highly relevant to the team in certain contingencies. You are seeking flexible people, not narrow specialists; those who can turn their minds and hands to a variety of problems with confidence.

'Nobody's Perfect but a Team can be'

How to design and construct a team that *simultaneously* meets the requirements of both functional and team roles constitutes one of the most intriguing aspects of teambuilding. This is also one of the most critical factors determining the fortunes of management teams in industry. It is here that the Marks and Spencer experience of team work offers the most valuable insight.

In a significant sense the effectiveness of the M & S management teams linger on the company's success in enabling most of its staff to have a relatively high degree of versatility in terms of functional as well as team roles. The M & S staff are to a considerable extent 'generalist' in both dimensions. This makes it possible to combine and recombine teams. This is perhaps another aspect of what Robert Keller has referred to as the 'inimitable magic' of M & S. But if our analysis has been substantially correct, then maybe it is not as mystic as the word 'magic' implies – though nonetheless 'inimitable'.

The M & S investment in training and in creating the conditions for effective team work has been gigantic and amazingly long-term, but the payoff, as we have seen, is equally spectacular. In practical business terms it enables the company to acquire a unique competitive edge which goes a long way to explaining the enviable record of the company's success.

From K.K. Tse, *Marks & Spencer: Anatomy of Britain's Most Efficiently Managed Company*, Pergamon, 1985

Ability to work as a team member

In selecting dogs during trials for teams of huskies to cross Antarctica, the explorers eliminated two kinds of dog: the *non-workers* and the *disruptives*. There is a parable here for human teams. Your selection process should discover those who are not motivated – they do not *want* to achieve, they do not strive to be in the team, and they will not work hard in harness or as individuals. Like the proverbial rotten apple, such individuals will have a bad influence on the rest of the group.

Some people, however, may not appear to be well motivated, possibly because they have worked too long under uninspiring leaders in lack lustre groups. But the fire is in the flint.

John Saunders was sixty, five years away from retirement. As an academic he had produced nothing. The head of a newly-established Department of Industrial History accepted the suggestion that Saunders should join him. 'Hard luck' said his present head, 'Saunders is just a deadbeat'. Yet in the lively and enthusiastic company of six younger colleagues, all publishing books and articles, Saunders came alive. In the next ten years he wrote seven books on industrial history.

The story of Saunders illustrates how others can inspire or motivate us. Find out if the potential is there before you discard someone on the grounds of motivation.

The second sort of person to leave on one side are those who will not make good team members because they are disruptive.

Harmony in groups is fragile enough as it is, without such liabilities as a naturally disruptive personality.

The key question to ask yourself and others relates to this factor: Is this person capable of functioning as a member of a high-performance team? If he is essentially a loner, or so

highly individualistic that he cannot subordinate his ego to the
common good, you will be wise to leave him to his own
devices.

It is not easy or necessary to analyse too closely what
constitutes this general capacity for working with others. So
much depends upon the other people involved in *this* team.
You have to be sensitive to the chemistry of the group.

The concept of *balance* is important here. Just as you do not
want an entire orchestra composed of clarinets or flutes, so you
do not want a team made up of introverts or extroverts,
analysts or creative thinkers.

Once you have eliminated the non-starters you should learn
as much as you can about each individual candidate. Then
make your judgement in terms of the chemistry and balance of
the group.

Interviews are a fairly blunt instrument for such team
selection. It is infinitely preferable, if it can be arranged, to see
the person in action with other members of the proposed
team. If that is not possible you can possibly see them at work
in another team, or at least talk to someone who has witnessed
them working in groups.

For individuals soon acquire a track record among colleagues, as they do with bosses and subordinates. The best
people to tell you about someone's capacity as a team member
are those who have worked in harness with him on some other
project.

Desirable personal attributes

So far you have thought about the person in terms of their
technical or professional ability and their fitness for the role of
team member. In both areas you are looking for a certain
standard. If you have in mind the formation of an exceptional
team, as opposed to a merely ordinary one, you will be seeking
technical skills of a high order, ones which interlock with the
contributions of other members of the team.

By now you will also have eliminated those with the roots of
two kinds of problems in them. Those who lack the basic
motivation to work hard are bound to become problems for
you, because their fellows in the team – intent upon high
performance – will turn against them. If you select those who
have a tendency to put up people's backs by their manner,

conversation or behaviour, you can be sure they will cost you a great deal of time later on. Apart from the thankless task of trying to develop them – no one can turn a dandelion into a rose, however much fertiliser you use – you will expend time smoothing down the ruffled feathers of group meetings, reconciling and harmonising like a diplomat.

Granted you are satisfied on technical grounds, and you know this person is not going to behave so as to disrupt the atmosphere you are trying to build, what are the desirable extra attributes you should look for?

In a sense this whole book is designed to help you form an accurate concept of the kind of person who will work well in a team. He or she will be someone who can contribute to the *process* skills of achieving the task – especially in the areas of decision making, problem solving and creative or innovative thinking – not merely contributing from a knowledge-base to the *content* of those decisions.

Desirable attributes, if not essential ones, include the ability to listen to others and to build on their contributions. That implies a flexibility of mind. The person who is too possessive about their own 'territory' or information is setting limits to his own and to the group's growth as a team.

Such flexibility implies a certain lack of suspicion. The ability both to give and to inspire trust is related to integrity, which may be defined as wholeness of character and adherence to standards – professional and moral – beyond oneself. If you appoint someone to your team who lacks integrity, whatever their professional competence or superficial social 'interactive skills', you are taking a big risk.

Last on the list, but still desirable, come such factors as likeability or popularity of a person. Members of teams are able to suppress quite intense personal dislikes for each other over the duration of the team's working life, and being likeable to everyone is not essential. But evidence suggests that children learn better from teachers they like. On that analogy it seems fairly obvious that adults will work better with colleagues they like. Provided, of course, that personal relations do not interfere with work relations, they surely enhance all human enterprise.

CHECKLIST:
HAVE YOU SELECTED THE RIGHT TEAM MEMBER?

Task   YES   NO

Has s/he an alert intelligence?   ☐   ☐

Where applicable, has s/he a high level of
vocational skills?   ☐   ☐

Do his or her knowledge/skills complement
those of other team members rather than
duplicate them?   ☐   ☐

Is s/he motivated to seek excellence in results
and methods of working together?   ☐   ☐

Does his or her track record really bear out the
scores given above?   ☐   ☐

Team

Will s/he work closely with others in decision-
making and problem solving without 'rubbing
people up the wrong way'?   ☐   ☐

Does s/he listen?   ☐   ☐

Is s/he flexible enough to adopt different roles
within the group?   ☐   ☐

Can s/he influence others – assertive rather than
aggressive?   ☐   ☐

Will s/he contribute to group morale rather than
draw cheques upon it?   ☐   ☐

Individual

Has s/he a sense of humour and a degree of
tolerance for others?   ☐   ☐

Has s/he a certain amount of will to achieve
ambition, tinged with understanding that s/he
cannot do it all alone?   ☐   ☐

Will s/he develop a feeling of responsibility for
the success of the team as a whole, not simply his
or her own part in it?   ☐   ☐

Has s/he integrity?   ☐   ☐

Does s/he have a realistic perception of his/her
strengths and weaknesses?   ☐   ☐

TEAMBUILDING EXERCISES

The phrase 'teambuilding exercises' may be new but the reality is not. Its origins go back at least as far as the medieval tournaments. These provided knights with military training and the opportunity to make reputations. Individual jousting and hand-to-hand combat came first. Then there were team events. In these a group of knights fought against another group. These teams often stayed together and fought side-by-side in real battle. Team games today, such as football, baseball, cricket and hockey, are the distant descendants of such medieval tournaments.

A crucial event in the movement from being a group to becoming a team can be the teambuilding exercise. This can be based upon either (1) a substitute team task (for example, a business case study or a few days of out-door activities or (2) a real task (for example, going away for a weekend to plan company strategy).

There are pros and cons to both approaches. The advantage of a substitute task type of event is that success or failure is not of paramount importance. Nor are there any technological or professional challenges to meet, so that people can concentrate on the essential issue of learning how to work more effectively together as a team. The disadvantage (apart from expense) is that the activities during the event can be perceived as games with little or no relevance to the job in hand. Moreover, at a certain level of seniority, managers become less willing to learn through this medium.

The real task has the obvious advantage of reality and immediacy. But the danger is that people become so immersed in it that the training objective is lost.

How does a leader navigate his way through those difficulties? He knows that having assembled individuals into a new group he has not yet acquired a team. For a team has to be grown or built through the experience of working together.

If time allows he can run training sessions for the group, which will have as one objective learning to work as an effective team. The tasks in these sessions may well be of the 'substitute task variety' – outdoor exercises or building towers with lego bricks for profit. But they should never be trivial or totally irrelevant. They should also be seen as introductory to tasks which closely resemble the actual tasks which the group

will be called upon to tackle together. The natural climax is
the group's first real task.

REVIEWING

In teambuilding exercises careful briefing about the object is
vital. Then the key part played by the *review* after the trial
runs needs to be stressed. This can be unstructured. You can
simply get the group together and ask 'How did the job go?
Could we have worked better as a team?'.

More often than not, with able managers or staff, the
general discussion that follows such open-ended questions will
cover all the points that the leader already has in mind. The
process of reflection, digesting experience and relating it to
principles, has begun. The important point is to build into the
programme opportunities for this unhurried reviewing or
looking back on the day's work together.

A more structured approach can be followed, using ques-
tionnaires or checklists which individuals complete and then
discuss. These certainly have a place, if used appropriately, in
getting a group to think critically about itself. They are
especially useful if a group is unaware of the real level of its
performance, or is disguising itself from some of the problems
within its life it can and should be solving. The results of a
checklist can then provide it with some hard evidence to chew
upon.

The reviewing phase in the teambuilding activity is not
temporary. A highly effective team is characterised by its
tendency towards regular and searching self-evaluation of
performance. Reviewing is an essential part of the process of
being a high-performance team.

For reviewing (and self-evaluation) to become a central
feature of team work, certain standards have to be set and
maintained. Reviewing should establish the facts first. What
was our objective? Did we in fact achieve it? If we did not, in
what ways did we fail?

Then you can come to *diagnosis*, introduced by the question
why. '*Why* did we succeed or not succeed?'. Analysis of the
reasons for success or failure will start in the task circle. Was
the goal clear? Did we have a workable plan? Was it com-
municated? Did we act flexibly, possibly altering the plan, in
the face of serious difficulty? And so on.

Then you should ask questions about the teamwork circle. 'How well did we work as a team?' Here questions-and-discussion should range over co-ordination and co-operation, group standards (technical and social), communication, atmosphere, changes in morale, the presence or absence of mutual encouragement.

Thirdly, any deficiencies in individual skills should be explored to identify training which will remedy them. You should be careful, as a general rule, not to criticise individuals in front of the group. Remember that you are *appraising* performance, not acting as a negative critic, so you will point out the good as well as the not-so-good points.

Teambuilding exercises, especially if they involve one or two nights away together, provide opportunities for *developing informal relationships*. Over a drink in the bar or the meal table, team members can get to know each other better. They compare their different as well as similar perspectives. What are consciously and carefully listened to are the theories, attitudes, worries, values and political concerns that members of the team have about the nature, causes and consequences of the current situation. Such discussion allows members of a team to see the *complexity* of the different strands of wisdom and desires of the team and allows that complexity to be ordered or negotiated through careful discussion.

It is important for you as leader to set a high standard of listening in these informal sessions. Reflections on issues and careful exploration of individual views implies a philosophy of teamwork which is far removed from the various 'instant teamwork' recipes offered on one day courses to managers. In many organisations people are encouraged to have as few meetings as possible and to get on with the 'real work'. But work which ignores individual values and perspectives can lead to superficial activity. In such low-performance teams, members are not committed to the activity, and the quality of the team's life is not enriched by the range of experience available within it.

THE ROLE OF CONSULTANT

In teambuilding exercises there is no doubt that the right consultant can play a significant part as a catalyst. He should not usurp the role of the leader, the person who owns the problem of developing *this* group into a team. His role – as an outsider – is complementary to the leader's one. His very presence can be a symbol and reminder of the training or development nature of the event.

Why, then, are consultants not more widely used to develop the effective teams that industry, commerce and the public services so sorely need?

Generally, consultants in this field have approached teambuilding from a background of T-group or sensitivity training. They have imported all the assumptions of the Group Dynamics movement into their work, including all these faulty assumptions about leadership. Inevitably this has led to a resistance to their message from practical managers, followed often by an outward rejection of what appears to be the old group dynamics approach.

But light is dawning. In an article entitled 'Second Thoughts on Team Building' two British consultants, Bill Critchley and David Casey, questioned the value and assumptions which underlie what is often called teambuilding and ultimately their usefulness in certain settings:

Teambuilding: At What Price and At Whose Cost?

It all started during one of those midnight conversations between consultants in a residential workshop. We were running a teambuilding session with a top management group and something very odd began to appear. Our disturbing (but also exciting) discovery was that for most of their time this group of people had absolutely no need to work as a team; indeed the attempt to do so was causing more puzzlement and scepticism than motivation and commitment. In our midnight reflections we were honest enough to confess to each other that this wasn't the first time our teambuilding efforts had cast doubts on the very validity of teamwork itself, within our client groups.

We admitted that we had both been working from some implicit assumptions that good teamwork is a characteristic of healthy, effectively functioning organisations. Now we started to question those assumptions. First, we flushed out what our assumptions actually were. In essence it came down to something like this:

We had been assuming that the top group in any organisation (be it the board of directors or the local authority management committee or whatever the top group is called) should be a team and ought to work as a team. Teamwork at the top is crucial to organisational success, we assumed.

We further assumed that a properly functioning team is one in which:

- people care for each other
- people are open and truthful
- there is a high level of trust
- decisions are made by consensus
- there is strong team commitment
- conflict is faced up to and worked through
- people really listen to ideas and to feelings
- feelings are expressed freely
- process issues (task and feelings) are dealt with

Finally, it had always seemed logical to us, that a teambuilding catalyst could always help any team to function better – and so help any organisation perform better as an organisation. Better functioning would lead the organisation to achieve its purposes more effectively.

The harsh reality we now came up against was at odds with this cosy view of teams, teamwork and teambuilding. In truth the Director of Education has little need to work in harness with his fellow chief officers in a county council. He or she might need the support of the Chief Executive and the Chair of the elected members' Education Committee, but the other chief officers in that local authority have neither the expertise nor the interest, nor indeed the time, to contribute to what is essentially very specialised work.

Even in industry, whilst it is clear that the marketing and production directors of a company must work closely together to ensure that the production schedule is synchronised with sales forecasts and the finance director needs to be involved – to look at the cash flow implications of varying stock levels – they don't need to involve the *whole* team. And they certainly do not need to develop high levels of trust and openness to work through those kinds of business issues.

On the other hand, most people would agree that *strategic* decisions, concerned with the future direction of the whole enterprise, should involve all those at the top. Strategy should demand an input from every member of the top group, and for strategic discussion and strategic decision-making, teamwork at the top is essential. But how much time do most top management groups actually spend discussing strategy? Our experiences, in a wide variety of organisations, suggest that 10 per cent is a high figure for most organisations – often 5 per cent would be nearer the mark. This means that 90-95 per cent of decisions in organisations are essentially operational; that is decisions made within departments based usually on a fair amount of information and expertise. In those conditions, high levels of trust and openness may be nice, but are not necessary; consensus is strictly not an issue and in any case would take up far too much time. There is therefore no need for high levels of interpersonal skills.

Why then, is so much time and money invested in teambuilding, we asked ourselves. At this stage in our discussions we began to face a rather disturbing possibility. Perhaps the spread of teambuilding has more to do with teambuilders and *their* needs and values rather than a careful analysis of what is appropriate and necessary for the organisation. To test out this alarming hypothesis we each wrote down an honest and frank list of reasons why we ourselves engaged in teambuilding. We recommend this as an enlightening activity for other teambuilders – perhaps, like us, they will arrive at this kind of conclusion; teambuilders work as catalysts to help management groups function better as open teams for a variety of reasons, including the following:

- They like it – enjoy the risks.
- Because they are good at it.
- It's flattering to be asked.

- They receive rewarding personal feedback.

- Professional kudos – not many people do teambuilding with top teams.

- There's money in it.

- It accords with their values: for instance democracy is preferred to autocracy.

- They gain power. Process interventions are powerful in business settings where the client is on home ground and can bamboozle the consultant in business discussions.

All those reasons are concerned with the needs, skills and values of the *teambuilder* rather than the management group being 'helped'. This could explain why many teambuilding exercises leave the so-called 'management team' excited and stimulated by the experience, only to find they are spending an unnecessary amount of time together discussing other people's departmental issues. Later on, because they cannot see the benefit of working together on such issues, they abandon 'teamwork' altogether. Such a management group has been accidentally led to disillusionment with the whole idea of teamwork and the value of teambuilding.

We began to see, as our discussions went on through the small hours, that there is a very *large* proportion of most managers' work where teamwork is not needed (and to attempt to inculcate teamwork is dysfunctional). There is at the same time a very *small* proportion of their work where teamwork is absolutely vital (and to ignore teamworking skills is to invite disaster). This latter work, which demands a team approach, is typified by strategic work but not limited to strategic work. It is any work characterised by a high level of choice and by the condition of maximum uncertainty.[21]

The authors discovered that fundamental issue, one which we have earlier explored in some depth: Do we need to be a team? The nature of some tasks does not appear to call for team work.

But, as we have seen, there is a complementary truth to be borne in mind in the teambuilding context. Although there are tasks that do not strictly demand team work it does make a difference if they are tackled by a team. In other words, if there is a team it will approach these tasks in a different way from a mere collection of individuals. Refer back to the three circles (p. 62). The task and team (and individual) circles are interactive. Although the task may require a certain structure in the group (team, organisation) area, so also the nature of the group (especially if it is working as a team) will effect the perception, definition and ultimately the accomplishment of the task.

The Sales Force

International Biscuits divided the country into two sales regions, North and South, each further subdivided into territories allocated to individual salesmen. In the South the Sales Manager held no meetings. He made the salesmen communicate directly to him, not to each other. 'I am the hub of the wheel', he told them. As the salesmen were constantly reminded that they were competing against each other they did not pass to each other relevant information about sales or customers.

The Northern Sales Manager generated a group *esprit de corps* among his salesmen. He constantly referred at their regular meetings to the value of co-operation, working as a team. Significant successes were shared by all. Salesmen would invite their neighbours into their territories if sudden large opportunities for business warranted it. Information was shared laterally by telephone as well as to the Sales Manager. In which sales region would you prefer to work?

A good consultant can help a group see possibilities of at least a degree of teamwork in what seems to be a mere assemblage of individual tasks or contributions. Iain Mangham, in an article entitled 'Building an effective work team',[22] gives a case study derived from his work as a consultant in an organisation where the management by objectives approach had been introduced with lack of the expected results.

Teamwork Development in Action

The section consisted of eight people, ranging from a leader with a PhD and considerable experience, to a process trainee with no qualifications and only a few weeks' experience of the company to draw on. All meetings were held at the works.

Before the first meeting, each member had filled out the questionnaire and added his comments. It was intended that this data should be organised and fed back anonymously, but the members felt there was little to be gained by this and a great deal to be lost by people not owning their scores. A ground rule was agreed whereby people were not to be pressured to explain their scores if they didn't wish to and, with this proviso, answers were shared.

It came as a surprise to most members to discover that there was considerable difference in answers.

The next few hours were spent in working through the scores. Why had discrepancies arisen? What specific events had shaped the respective images of the team? There was an initial reluctance to focus on the section itself; frequently scores were justified by examples drawn from outside groups – experiences in other teams in the department, experiences with other leaders in other teams at other times, but gradually the members began to talk about their current feelings, their own team, their experiences in it and the problems they had in its effective operation.

At the outset there was a marked degree of scepticism about working as a section team at all.

'I do my job and he does his, but I'm damned if there's any reason why I should go out of my way to help him.'

'There's no reason for us to have contact, we don't need each other . . .'

'There's not one team here, there's three or four – in some instances eight.'

Comments such as these led to considerable discussion about what benefits, if any, could accrue from operating together rather than in twos or threes. A consensus was reached which accepted that whilst it was impossible and, perhaps, undesirable to find out completely what others were engaged in, there was certainly a great deal to be gained from sharing information more fully and from sharing responsibilities more widely through the section.

A great deal of time was spent on this issue because it was considered to be the most fundamental. If there were to be latent feelings that operating as a team was not meaningful then the rest of the training would be irrelevant. In inviting the members to discuss this issue the consultant was epitomising the approach to be stressed throughout the training, that the working-through of problems was essential to effective relationships.

The above case illustrates the value of having a consultant present to act as a change agent or catalyst. But his role should always be subordinate and complementary to that of the team leaders. For the latter *owns* the problem of teambuilding in this situation, not the outsider. As always with consultants, use them selectively and sparingly.

In conclusion, the first objective in teambuilding is to choose the right people in the light of the team's purpose. Then you should aim at developing a group identity. Giving the team a name and a base or place to meet are important steps in that direction. In the early meetings it is helpful to remember that the new members – who may know you well but not each other – are coming with the following questions in mind:

Why are we in this group?

Do we need to work as a team?

Even if it is not necessary would it benefit us to do so?

Are we going to collaborate or compete?

Are our objectives realistic?

How are decisions to be made?

How is our performance to be appraised?

How are we going to grow in effectiveness?

POINTS TO PONDER

Team work is required by many tasks; even where it is not strictly needed working as a team can transform performance and enhance job satisfaction. Good teams are not the products of chance. As a leader, one of your three major responsibilities is to build the team.

If you are assembling a new team concentrate on selecting individual members who will use complementary skills, techniques and knowledge and also build up the common life. Look for those with extra qualities of personality and character mentioned above.

Within the first year of its life try to get your team away for a day or two on its own. With the help of a varied programme of tasks and events – practical activities followed by review – identify with them the strengths and weaknesses of the team, listing the areas for improvement. Return home with an action plan for moving from low- to high-performance team levels.

The power of a team to accomplish its mission is directly related to how well the leader selects and develops its members

CASE STUDY: TEAMBUILDING IN BECHTEL GREAT BRITAIN LIMITED

Garth Ward, Project Manager, describes here one approach to creating a team in a project-based industry operating within a matrix-type of organisation.

All organisational structures have communication problems and if it isn't the organisation itself then the language and individuals certainly create a communication problem. To overcome this you need a fairly conventional type of organisation and for project-based industries I think the most successful is a task force where all the team members are physically located together in one area. This helps to give an identity to the team and it needs a team to get anything done. Members are selected from the line management structure of the company. Within this team, the members receive their day-to-day instructions from the project manager. The functional manager, who has provided the resources, produces a system of checks and balances so as to audit the quality of the work. As you can see, in a project-based industry everybody has two bosses: the project manager, and the functional manager. This creates conflict since the team members know that they will be working for their functional managers once the project has come to an end. So how does the project manager provide the necessary motivation? One way is for the project manager to share in the responsibilities for the performance evaluation of his team. There can be no better way to motivate an individual's productivity than for him to know that his day-to-day performance is being assessed by someone who has a real say on his pay, promotion and next assignment. The interest and support that can be demonstrated by executive management is also vital. Then, if we have got our Herzberg Hygiene Factors right, we can start motivating through the project manager in building up team spirit.

Teambuilding for a successful project is not just about the lead members of a project management group. Teambuilding goes right through the project, to include the client, the vendors, the subcontractors and the manual workforce on the jobsite. All of these have to be approached in different ways, because they all have different problems. One of the main reasons for teambuilding is to reduce the conflict in the matrix organisation. The most pronounced example of this is in the relationship between the home office and the construction group. This arises primarily from lack of awareness that the plant is not about the design on the drawing board, but it is about how you build it in the field. It is the construction people who have the primary input into the planning exercise and unless you integrate them into your home office team, you will produce or enhance conflict between construction and engineering.

The modern construction manager to look for is the one who is intelligent and far-sighted enough to avoid problems, but, who also has the ability to solve field problems. Unfortunately, site managers have not been known for their teambuilding skills. They have usually solved their problems by bringing in a few good people whom they know and trust and whom they have identified over the years as the people who are going to make the job a success for them. In fact they bypass any teambuilding by bringing in elements of a ready-made team and leave the remainder to knuckle under through fear of having their assignment contract terminated.

It is because the construction manager also identifies his boss as the functional construction department manager that you have this conflict between the site construction manager and the project manager, who has the responsibility of delivering the project on time.

I know this to be true from my own experience when I worked overseas as a resident project manager on the same site as the construction manager. In this situation you have the constitutional monarch (the project manager) who has in theory all of the executive power, but is not able to exercise it; and the prime minister (the site manager) who in theory works for the executive, who has the direct application of all the *real* power. Not a happy combination on a construction site! For these reasons I like to integrate the site manager into the home office team as early as possible in order to build up relationships within the team.

I believe that teambuilding starts at the proposal stage, because that is when the project manager gets the rest of the team to develop and buy-into his plan. You also get a tremendous 'welding together' when that particular proposal team starts to prepare their presentation to the client. This requirement for a presentation is a trend which is occurring more and more often and I suspect that it is not out of any desire by the client to build a team, but rather to enable him to find the difference between the various bids. These days we are all professional and competitive with our bids and clients need new criteria to find some way of separating them. It is this presentation exercise that starts to develop the real beginnings of a team spirit.

In addressing the problem of how the contractor and client work towards the same objectives, I would like to start by looking at the bidding selection process. This is surely the area where the client makes his most momentous decision. Before, I reluctantly came to the conclusion that the competitive bidding process was necessary because there was no other means of selecting a meaningful contractor. I would now revise that opinion and say that it is identifying and achieving the client's objectives of cost and schedule that are the real measure of success. Unfortunately, the client too often takes the easy way out and, because market conditions indicate that he can squeeze the contractor for that little bit extra, he goes for lump sum contracts. He can, regrettably, get himself into the situation where the contractor is squeezed that little bit too much. To quote John Ruskin in 1860, 'It is unwise to pay too much, but it's worse to pay too little. When you pay too much, you lose a little money – that's all. When you pay too little, you sometimes lose everything, because the thing you bought was incapable of doing the thing it was bought to do. The common law of business balance prohibits paying a little and getting a lot – it can't be done. If you deal with the lowest bidder it is well to add something for the risk you run. And if you do that, you will have enough to pay for something better'. He was a very wise man . . .

The client chooses the lump sum contract route, to ensure that the contractor is motivated; however, too often it has the opposite effect because the contractor ends up looking for all the various ways of cutting corners in order to save himself some money.

What the client really wants is a contractor who will make an effort to improve productivity in the field and yet, in the evaluation process, any impact that the contractor may have in this area is eliminated by the client doing his comparison on normalised manhours (so as to remove the element of cheating by the various bidders).

The real way to motivate the contractor is to structure a sensible bonus-sharing scheme (between client and contractor) whereby the contractor enhances his profit by beating mutually agreed goals on schedule, fabrication progress, safety standards, etc.

Clients should evaluate the contractor's commitment to teambuilding and success with teambuilding (by success, I mean the ultimate productivity improvement in the field and the bringing of projects in on schedule and under budget); couple that with a bonus incentive scheme and you can have a happy client who has control of the situation, and at the same time has a strongly motivated contractor.

Once the project is awarded there are two elements to teambuilding: the first one is the straightforward getting together of the team to plan the job. This must be a very detailed stage. It is during these discussion and argument sessions that relationships are formed by the lead members and you get the same relationships being built with the client by your regular progress meetings.

Secondly, you need to create an artificial environment to bridge some of those gaps which are caused by lack of awareness and knowledge of individual people. It is for these sessions that I believe in using some form of training specialist as a facilitator to make sure that things do not get out of hand. It is here I suppose that teambuilding becomes somewhat of a science rather than the art that I believe it is.

Let us look at an approach that we used on a practical problem on a UK job site, where some of the issues were similar to those in the NEDO report of the late 1970s 'What's wrong on site?' I would like to compare our approach to achieving a smooth running Rugby Union fifteen in formation, between the pack, the half backs and the three-quarters. Our training manager, Roger Griffin, started with the construction manager and his direct reports. We spent two days off the job looking at what was in it for each of the individuals and what their personal goals were. We had a series of exercises to allow individuals to become more familiar with each other's values, using the classic John Adair leadership game, the Lego bricks, and we introduced an element of competition. Then we looked at what the project was about and what were the key milestones they were trying to achieve. We also involved our client in this to build up project relationships for joint success and remove any 'win/lose' competition between the two project managers.

There was an overriding issue at this particular site, namely the power and influence of the local trade unions, versus the foreman and the first line supervision. The exercise which we got the team to work on was planning on how to redress that balance. As our next step we looked at building-up the relationship between the next higher level of supervision, the superintendents and the field engineers. Both of these groups had been in the company for quite some time but they had not actually worked together before. So we mixed straightforward training with teambuilding. We covered things like industrial relations, safety standards and assertiveness, and the whole exercise culminated in a one-day role play where we reconstructed an industrial relations tribunal case.

We asked this group to contribute to the plan for training the foremen as our last exercise where we undertook a four-day training programme for the foremen. We covered the same subjects: industrial relations, safety, planning and scheduling the site agreement, and assertiveness. We integrated the superintendent group at this stage with some case studies. The willingness of the foremen to get involved was shown by the fact that they gave up part of their weekend for this particular exercise.

We then evaluated how well we had done half-way through the project by means of a two-day group exercise reviewing successes and failure. The bottom line was a direct contribution of a seven-week schedule improvement and an indirect saving to the client, at a conservative estimate, of £250,000.

Earlier I indicated that other parties to the project, for example vendors and subcontractors, should not be ignored in the teambuilding exercise. On a recent project, I had two very significant multi-million pound vendors who were vital to the success of the project. One was a good old fashioned British company making a standard product and I felt delighted that I would not have any problems in this area. The other was to be a tailor made product by what I thought would be one of those wilful continental vendors, a recipe for problems. Strangely enough, the complete opposite happened. We failed to get the British vendor to identify with our objectives and he stuck firmly to his objective of not putting more efforts into his contract than he would for a normal standard product. Consequently, we had no end of problems due to unfinished work. The continental vendor, on the other hand, identified very firmly with our objectives, particularly when we introduced a bonus scheme, and despite having all kinds of problems thrown in his path the result was a high quality product completed ahead of schedule.

How the contractor and client get along on site depends upon the contractual arrangement. With a lump sum contract only the objective of completing on schedule is really common to both the client and the contractor. If the contractor wants to stay in business he also has the objective of completing under his budget. Unfortunately, this is the overriding motivating factor so that completing on schedule may not actually be common to both of them. If the contractor believes in all the good things we have been talking about he will perform in a similar manner. Good teambuilding produces good IR, good safety and good productivity, so it should not cost him any more. This situation is perhaps more difficult in dealing with subcontractors on site, since they have not been involved in the actual development of any plan, but have had it imposed upon them. This is why the pre-commitment induction meeting for subcontractors is so important. Basically there should be no difference in the way one manages a contract. The client's money should be looked after as effectively on a reimbursable contract as on a lump sum contract. The difference comes in his involvement. In the lump sum contract he has little or no influence (or he should not be allowed any), thus making it an easy job for the project manager. Whereas on the reimbursable contract he makes the project manager's job difficult because he wants to get involved in all the decisions without accepting any of the responsibility.

One client I know has solved the problem of how to

establish common goals in a scenario that goes something like this: 'How are you going to improve or tackle the problem of poor productivity on spool fabrication?' Note that at this stage he does not give you any of his own ideas, because he does not want to be seen to be giving any instructions or guidance, so that he can be laid open to claim and blame later on. The contractor goes away and thinks of, say, three plans, and because he has done this exercise before he thinks of all the pro's and con's. He has it thoroughly evaluated and then presents it to the client. The client considers it and comes back with a whole bunch of questions and counter-arguments which really knock the contractor's plan. However, the contractor gives way and modifies his plan and this to-ing and fro-ing goes on for about two or three weeks. Ultimately, in desperation, the contractor grabs at any indications he can from the client, until he thinks, 'At last I have second-guessed what the client's plan really is'. So he implements it, because he thinks he has agreement from the client, or rather he has not actually got disagreement. He really feels it is a rather second-rate plan. He knows his own plan would have worked well if he had implemented it when he had first suggested it. When something goes wrong, the contractor in total frustration, 'loses his cool' and tells the client, 'I told you it wouldn't work', only to be greeted with 'Well, it was your plan – *you* recommended it!'

This approach is unfortunate in that it reduces all plans to the lowest common denominator and prevents one taking advantage of the theory that an average plan, well implemented is better than a good plan badly implemented.

Teambuilding is something you have to believe in and to which you must be committed. You cannot expect to see the bottom line saving. You certainly will not be able to see a saving directly attributable to teambuilding, but it is the process of teambuilding that makes people communicate effectively. If they communicate effectively they will plan effectively and in doing this they will do the job right the first time. If you do the job right the first time, you get the greater enthusiasm and the increased productivity accordingly. To put it differently, you do not demotivate people by making them re-do work when they think they have just completed it. I can summarise my arguments as follows:

- Commitment to the company is achieved by making employees aware and participating in company decisions, but firstly you have to get your hygiene factors correct. Commitment to projects is achieved by the organisational structure created for that project, or in other words the team. It is the success and achievement on projects that enhances the commitment to the company.

- Tendering is the best stage at which to start teambuilding and is done most successfully by using the team to prepare the proposal and make the presentation to the client.

- The establishment of common goals on site is perhaps the most difficult area to address and needs to be tackled at various levels. The manual workforce performs better if the work goes together well without a lot of re-work when they have good direction. The foreman and supervisors can perform more effectively if top management has taken the trouble to identify goals by involving them in some of the decision-making processes.

- The client and management will perform more effectively if they have actually taken the trouble to get to know each other.

- The client's wish for control and management's need for autonomy is dependent upon the type of contract: a lump sum contract excluding client involvement and the reimbursable contract giving the client scope for absolute control or degrees of manipulation.

I end by referring to the following list of some well-recognised criteria for measuring success in teambuilding.

Phases of a Project

1 Enthusiasm

2 Disillusionment

3 Panic

4 Search for the guilty

5 Punishment of the innocent

6 Praise and honour for the non-participants.

How does one measure that success? I think it depends upon how many of these phases you go through. Maybe all projects go through the first three phases but if you get to 'Search for the guilty', you have certainly failed! Perhaps suitable criteria for finishing a successful project are:

- Evaluate the options
- Communicate the solutions
- Praise and honour to the team.

12 Creative problem solving

Preview of Chapter Twelve
- What is a problem?
- What mental processes are involved in successful problem solving?
- A framework for problem solving
- Brainstorming
- Follow up
- Your key role as leader
- Points to ponder

By no means all teams are required to sit down as a group to make decisions, solve problems or generate new ideas. In sports teams, for example, it may be the manager and the captain who make all the decisions, while individual players solve problems posed by the opposition and play with what flair they can. In an operating theatre team the surgeon in charge will make the key decisions; anything like creative thinking would probably be inappropriate.

In the context of management, however, a degree of team work is required both to make and implement the best decisions. That does not detract in any way from the accountability of the leader in charge. Like the surgeon, he must 'carry the can'. But if he is wise the manager will involve his team as far as possible in the decisions which affect their common work.

The reason for this policy is not only the obvious motivational one: the more that people participate in a decision the more they are motivated to carry it out. Each member of the team will bring a different experience, knowledge, imagination, perspective and judgement to bear upon the decision. As a result, it should be a better decision as well as a more acceptable one – providing the leader is a competent thinker himself and knows what is wanted.

To become more effective in this area a team should have shared frameworks, drills or maps for decision making and problem solving. This chapter identifies the key ones.

WHAT IS A PROBLEM?

Many people now use the phrases 'decision making' and 'problem solving' as if they were synonyms. The processes of deciding and solving do in fact overlap but there are distinctions between them.

A decision means, literally, a cut-off point. It is the point where you cut your stream of thought about some matter. The most common reason for cutting short your mental processes is because you have made up your mind to do – or not to do – something about the matter you have been considering.

Decision implies action. After you have deliberately taken action – or no action – there will be reactions from others and from the wider environment. Some of these results you can foresee: these can be called the *manifest consequences* of your act. There are others, however, which you cannot or did not foresee – the *latent consequences*.

Let us turn to problem solving. A problem means, literally, something thrown in front of you. That can range from a puzzle to a matter which requires a decision about appropriate action. It is another very general and much-used word. At the puzzle end of the spectrum, of course, a solution does not involve action or affect your life in the way a decision might. Therefore some people – many academics, for example – can be very good at solving intricate problems like the structure of genes or the sub-atomic nature of matter and yet hopeless at decision making. Equally, good decision makers may lack some of the necessary mental qualities required in a supreme puzzle-solver.

But a problem must be problematic. If you know the answer by direct recall of facts or the application of a readily-available technique you are not faced with a problem. (The exercise $27\sqrt{9842}$ is *not* a problem for a person with a calculator or one who knows how to perform long division). Therefore a problem is a task for which:

- The person or group confronting it wants or needs to find a solution

- The person or group has no readily available procedure for finding the solution

- The person or group must make an attempt to find a solution

This definition stresses the three essential components of a problem: (1) the motivation of the problem solvers to attain a goal; (2) the fact that the goal cannot be reached directly or immediately; and (3) the fact that a conscious effort to attain the goal is made.

The first component requires that leaders present the problems they want their teams to solve in a way sufficiently attractive for subordinates and colleagues to *want* to solve them. It is no good posing problems if the team members are not interested in attempting to solve them.

Members will probably not be able to get the solution immediately but they must feel it is within their grasp. Too often people believe that if a decision cannot be made quickly (or a problem solved speedily) it cannot be done at all. Nothing could be further from the truth!

Consequently leaders who intend to make problem solving a real part of teamwork must pay especial attention to the unique relationship that exists between task, group and individual. For they should be able to maintain morale in team and individual in the face of repeated failures to overcome a particular obstacle or to solve a thorny problem.

In the management context, creative thinking is best understood as one general method of problem solving. Here the novelty and unexpectedness of the course of action or solution adopted is such that we call it creativity.

To remind you of an earlier point teams, like committees – or teams in committee – are not themselves creative. It is individual members who have the bright ideas. But groups can provide a *context* in which creative thinking flourishes. Atmosphere, communication, standards, leadership, morale; all contribute to a positive climate which stimulates, triggers, encourages and develops the exploratory thinking of individuals.

WHAT MENTAL PROCESSES ARE INVOLVED IN SUCCESSFUL PROBLEM SOLVING?

Before describing a *framework* for a team to have consciously in mind when tackling problems, I want to outline the mental processes which come into play in successful problem solving.

Problem solving is integrating your previous experience and knowledge together with your natural mental skill in an attempt to resolve a situation whose outcome is not known. To make progress the group or team, like the individual problem solver, must have sufficient motivation and lack of stress or anxiety. Progress made will in itself fuel the fires of motivation.

Fig. 12.1 helps explain why an individual or group with all necessary knowledge to solve a problem may still fail to do so. High stress levels, lack of desire or interest and unfamiliarity with the appropriate strategies or procedures for tackling that

Personality factors	*Experience factors*	*Cognitive factors*
stress, pressure	age	memory
interest, motivation	previous professional/ technical background	analytical ability
anxiety to perform		logic and reasoning
resistance to premature closure	familiarity with solution – finding strategies	synthesising ability
perseverance		valuing ability
	familiarity with problem content and context	holistic
		imaginative
		intuition, flair
		numeracy, literacy

Fig. 12.1   Some Factors that influence the Problem-Solving Process

sort of issue are some of the obstacles which can slow down
progress or ultimately prevent success.

The last chapter, on selecting team members, covered many
of the factors listed under Personality and Experience. Here I
shall concentrate on the Cognitive factors – the basic mental
skills given by nature, shaped by education and sharpened by
training.

My argument is that we each have a profile of strengths and
weaknesses in these mental abilities. The Complete Thinker –
the Thinker for All Seasons – would have them all in an
outstanding degree, but he is a rare bird. Most of us are better
at one or two kinds of thinking than the rest. Therefore it
stands to reason that if you are building a team of ten members
which has applied thinking as part of its task you do not want
ten superb analysers and no synthesisers or evaluators. Otherwise you will end up with paralysis by analysis. The principle
of balance applies.

Setting aside personality and experience or knowledge
considerations, what are the prime mental skills you should be
seeking to include within the team? The following are the
main ones:

- *Analysing* The capacity to take things apart, to separate
  out, to divide a problem into sections, to
  distinguish the central from the peripheral, to
  place things or people into categories, to
  dissect the complex into its constituent parts.

- *Reasoning* The ability (related to analytical thinking) to
  think in logical steps, usually from the
  general to the particular (deduction) or from
  the particular to the general (induction).

- *Synthesising* The reverse process of analysing, namely the
  putting together of parts into a whole,
  assembling pieces of a jigsaw into a complete
  picture, placing things together so they work.

- *Holistic thinking* The tendency to see the whole rather than the
  parts, especially the way in which the whole is
  more than the sum of the parts. (Note that
  holistic thinkers tend to be hostile to overmuch analysis, for the properties of the whole
  disappear under analysis. They are inclined
  to natural analogies, such as growth).
  Visionaries are often holistic.

- *Valuing*

The capacity to value accurately according to appropriate scales of worth. This is obviously conditioned by the content and context of the valuing activity, for example, valuing diamonds. But there is a more general valuing ability, for example, over people, summed up by the word *judgement*. (Note that highly evaluative people can be hypercritical of ideas, others and themselves – natural critics. The word critic comes from the Greek word for a judge).

- *Intuition*

The faculties of analysing, synthesising and valuing are exercised both consciously and subconsciously – in the depth mind. Intuition is one manifestation of the depth mind at work, suggesting conclusions or ideas or ways forward without any apparent conscious reasoning taking place. 'I have but a woman's reason – I think him so because I think him so', wrote Shakespeare. If shown consistently it is called flair.

- *Memory*

Memory is the most important active department of the depth mind: it is our library, storage and retrieval system. There is more in it than we know, hence the ideas or thoughts of others in discussion can unlock unknown boxes in our own memories. Note that if groups or teams stay together for any length of time they also acquire something like a corporate depth mind and memory. Sometimes they need to be reminded of what they have learnt already but have temporarily forgotten.

- *Creativity*

The ability, for example, to synthesise or relate together two or more ideas that appear to most people to be unconnected into a new whole. Note that there is a value judgement in creativity: others have to judge the new synthesis or idea creative rather than merely novel. Closely related to creativity is imagination: the ability to think in pictures.

- *Numeracy/ Literacy*

These describe the natural abilities to think in terms of numbers or words.

As a leader you should obviously try to sharpen your skills in these areas; they are fundamental in determining the quality of your thinking, which in turn will colour all your decisions. Elsewhere I have suggested ways of self-development in this area.[23]

Think now of each member – or would-be member – of your team. What is he going to bring to the party? What are his strengths? Does he know his limitations, so that he is willing to listen to and accept the contributions of others? Have you any notable mental ability under-represented in the team?

A FRAMEWORK FOR PROBLEM SOLVING

In making decisions and solving problems (and I am talking here about where those two concepts overlap) it is useful to have a shared method of going about things. It may be valuable in training for the team to be taught this as a drill, as is done on many standard management courses where the drill is first explained and then applied by course members to exercises and case studies. But the best soldiers, I was once told, are those who are thoroughly disciplined and drilled in training and then allowed to revert to their natural ferocious selves!

The classic framework or general strategy for decision making/problem solving involves five steps:

Activity	Notes
• defining the objective or problem	mainly analytical
• collecting data or reviewing the information already held	involves experience and memory as well as information-seeking or research skills, literacy (reading) and numeracy
• generating alternative feasible solutions or courses or action	mainly synthesising, but the word *feasible* implies an element of rough valuing
• choosing a right answer, or the optimum course of action	mainly valuing, usually in decision making using more than one criterion of value

- evaluating the decision   either before, during or after
  implementing it

The drawback of this framework, useful though it is, lies in the limitations of language. We have to use words like steps, stages or phases, which imply a logical step-by-step process with each stage tidily completed before the next commences. But thinking is not neat and tidy like that although it should always strive to be disciplined and orderly. In the actual process of thinking the mind may dart forwards and backwards. Gathering relevant information, for example, which is nominally the second phase, will probably occur in all the other phases in some shape or form.

Understanding the Problem

- Define the problem in your own words
- Decide what you are trying to do
- Identify important facts and factors

Solving the Problem

- check all main assumptions
- Ask questions
- List main obstacles
- Work backwards
- Look for a pattern

- List all possible solutions or ways
- Decide the criteria
- Narrow down to feasible solutions
- Select optimum one
- Agree implementation programme

Evaluating the decision and implementing it

- Be sure you used all the important information
- Check your proposed decision from all angles
- Ensure that plan is realistic
- Review decision in light of experience

Fig. 12.2   Problem-solving Guide

The nature of thinking therefore makes it exceptionally hard to lead a really effective team effort involving minds at work. Self-discipline on the part of members is essential. That will be helped if they are following a common problem solving strategy.

In the boardroom or upon many a committee much of this thinking will have been done by a sub-group or an individual commissioned to write a paper on the subject. Check that the paper obeys the ground rules that have been set for the team as a whole. Is the problem clearly stated? Is the relevant information there and is it accurately summarised? Are the feasible options set out? Do the authors make a recommendation – a tentative decision subject to approval?

Within the general framework of defining the objective or problem, generating feasible alternatives and choosing the best one, there are some more specific tactics worth bearing in mind.

The headings in Fig. 12.2 are mainly self-explanatory. Working backwards means trying to envisage the end state and then working out what needs to be done to get there. It requires a degree of imagination. Many chief executives use this strategy now when they ask their boards, 'Where do we want to be as a company in five years time?'

BRAINSTORMING

Brainstorming is a means of generating ideas from a group of people in a short time. It works best on simple but open-ended problems where there is no one answer like:

Finding a new name for a product

Getting more people into a shop

Getting more people to buy a product

Brainstorming is based upon the principle of deferred judgement, or, as expressed by its originator, Alex Osborn, the principle of suspended judgement.[24] The basis is deliberate alternation of the thought process. In other words, one should turn on his valuing mind at one time and his creative mind at another, instead of trying to think both critically and imaginatively at the same time.

Yet how many of us are prepared to suspend our critical or judgemental faculty altogether, simply for fear of making fools of ourselves?

Alex Osborn goes on to give three principles which provide the foundation for group brainstorming. First, idea listing can be more productive if criticism is concurrently excluded. This principle is considered important because education and experience have trained most adults to think judicially rather than creatively. Consequently, they tend to impede their fluency of ideas by applying their critical power too soon.

Second, the more ideas the better. Those who have had the most experience with brainstorming are practically unanimous in their agreement that in idea production quantity helps breed quality. And, third, group work to produce ideas can be more productive than an individual working on his own. Osborn refers to numerous experiments which show that, in the same length of time and under similar conditions, the average person can think up about twice as many ideas when working with a group as when working alone. These can be tabulated as in Fig. 12.3.

If the group falls silent during brainstorming allow silence to continue for a full two minutes before contributing. This procedure maintains time pressure as well as giving an opportunity for the individual's depth mind to work.

The following are examples of the sort of ideas, big and small, that can come from brainstorming, or genuinely judgement-free situations:

New ways to combat vandalism on buses

When brainstormed recently, ideas included personal name badges for conductors (so that they ceased to be anonymous representatives of authority), two-way radios, soothing background music, and unbreakable mirrors facing the front seats (so that people would be made aware of themselves).

New ways of saving energy

A heat recovery unit has been developed that uses the heat extracted from cows' milk to heat in turn the water for such processes as pipeline washing, udder washing, and calf feeding. It can reduce a dairy's electric water heating requirements by up to 60 per cent.

Suspend judgement	Criticism is ruled out. Adverse judgement of ideas must be withheld until later. Do not evaluate.
Free-wheel	Free-wheeling is welcomed. The wilder the idea, the better; it is easier to tame down than to think up. Let your mind drift.
Strive for quantity	Quantity is wanted. The greater the number of ideas, the more the likelihood of success. Aim at, say, a hundred ideas in a period of fifteen to thirty minutes.
Combine and improve	Combination and improvement are sought. In addition to contributing ideas of their own, participants should suggest how ideas of others can be turned into better ideas; or how two or more ideas can be joined into still another idea. Hitch-hike on other people's ideas.

Fig. 12.3   Four Rules for Group Brainstorming

New uses for household waste

A pilot scheme has recently been approved for the conversion of human sewage into animal feeding stuffs. The scheme, if applied commercially, could dramatically improve river and coastal waters, and save a great deal of the £250 million currently spent in the UK on imported feeding stuffs.

New ways of sending mail

'. . . A piece of paper just large enough to bear the stamp, covered at the back with a glutinous wash, which the sender might, by applying a little moisture, attach to the back of the letter . . .' An extract from the original proposal by Rowland

Hill, inventor of the postage stamp. When the then Postmaster General heard of it, he exploded: 'Of all the wild and visionary schemes I have ever heard of, or read of, this is the most extravagant!'

I have used brainstorming quite often on leadership training courses and during teambuilding exercises. One of the group is asked to act as recorder, since it has been found that listing of ideas as they are produced gives the group access to all of its output at all times, ensuring also that no ideas are lost. The recording method which works best is large scale (for example, using felt pens on flop chart paper or chalk on blackboards) so it is easily readable by everyone in the group. Brainstorming is most effective if the problem is simple and can be well-defined. But I have found it can contribute at all stages of more complex problem solving, from defining the problem to final details of implementation.

FOLLOW-UP

It has been demonstrated that not more than forty minutes should be allocated to the actual session but the participants are asked to go on considering the problem and send in further suggestions. These are added to the list already obtained and all ideas are classified into logical categories by the leader. These are handed to the person who submitted the problem initially. He then undertakes evaluation of the list, possibly processing ideas by combination, elaboration or additions of his own.

Evaluation may be best done not by the brainstorming group itself but by a small group of five members directly concerned with the problem. Keep the brainstorming group informed of the result, otherwise they may want to be excused the next time they are asked! The steps of evaluation are:

- Decide on appropriate criteria
- Pick out instant winners
- Eliminate the useless or inappropriate
- Sort similar ideas into groups and select best of each group

- Apply criteria to instant winners and best of each group
- Submit the short-list ideas to reverse brainstorming (that is, in how many ways can this idea fail?)

Although the main purpose of brainstorming is to generate ideas, there are many by-products which may be of considerable value. Brainstorming provides a means of finding out what people think about management problems; it helps people gain a better understanding of, and tolerance for, each other; it improves morale; it encourages initiative by making members more willing to accept and tackle problems; it increases confidence in their own abilities.

Exercise

To practise your team in creative problem solving, give them some problems to solve and appoint observers. Here is a specimen problem:

Thermos bottle: closure problem[25]
You are familiar with the wide-mouthed thermos bottle. The mouth is wide to permit the entrance of a spoon for eating stews, and so on. Imagine that you have been employed to invent a new closure for this product to replace the plug. The new closure must fall within the following specifications:

It should be loss-proof and integral with the bottle so that the top does not have to be removed to get at the contents.
No strings, chains, or hinges.
Closure must not depend on cup, so that user can reclose bottle while cup is in use.
The cup top should be retained in some usable form.
It must not add more than twenty per cent to the retail cost.
It must be easily cleaned.
It must be thermally effective for ten hours.
It must hold pressures up to 1½ pounds per square inch.
No basic change in the thermos bottle itself is acceptable.
The wide mouth must be retained.

As the team works on this exercise, you may find it useful to appoint one or two observers armed with the following checklist:

CHECKLIST

- Do the group members establish a common understanding of the problem, based upon a careful diagnosis?
- Do they focus together on a single aspect of the problem, or does each member have his own way of seeing the problem?
- Do they actually work as a team, building on each others' ideas, or as a group of individuals?
- Do the members take pains to make sure everyone understands each idea?
- Was the technical content of the discussion at a high level?
- Does anyone use analogies to suggest possible solutions?
- Do the members really listen to one another?
- Do the members tend to shoot down ideas quickly?
- Does the group insist that each idea be a complete solution?
- Or do they support and improve on an unsatisfactory idea?
- Do they thoroughly explore one idea before going on to the next?
- Did people keep to the point and not waste time? .

YOUR KEY ROLE AS LEADER

Leading a group meeting of any kind – committee or team – for the solution of a problem is a difficult job and requires both task and maintenance factors, as well as personal qualities of mind, personality and character.

Professor Norman Maier[26] wrote an article called 'Assets and Liabilities in Group Problem Solving' in which he made the following points:

- The skill of the leader requires his ability to create a climate for disagreement which will permit innovation without risking hard feelings.

- When the discussion leader aids the consideration of several aspects of the problem-solving process and delays the solution mindedness of the group solution, quality and acceptance improve.

- Problem-solving activity includes searching, trying out ideas on one another, listening to understand rather than to refute, making relatively short speeches and reacting to differences in opinion as stimulating.

- For a participative group to work the leader must concentrate on the group process, listen in order to understand rather than to appraise or refute, assume responsibility for accurate communication between members, be sensitive to unexpressed feelings, protect minority points of view, keep the discussion moving and develop skills in summarising.

In decision making (as opposed to many forms of problem solving) a leader will have to be concerned with the acceptability of the decision to those who will be implementing it. What degree of acceptability is required? Maier's model below illustrates the options:

Quality of Solution Required

		Low	High
Degree of acceptability required of those implementing decisions	*High*	Agreement needed but technical factors unimportant	Technical excellence and unanimity needed
	Low	Quick decision possible	Probable need for experts but not much discussion by others

Fig. 12.4   Maier's Model

Models like this are thought-provoking but they don't make decisions or solve problems. Only people meeting and agreeing upon a course of action or a solution can do that. However, too many meetings of groups and teams are badly led. For meetings are about people. Bringing intelligent and able people together inevitably means that contrasting views – if not conflicting or clashing ones – will be expressed. Your main asset as a leader is your skill in managing the resolution of different opinions and obtaining commitment to effective action.

POINTS TO PONDER

Success in problem solving requires effort directed at overcoming a surmountable obstacle. Use all available facts, inadequate as they are; seek more information if necessary as well as suggestions, clarifications and reactions. It is difficult to get away from preconceived ideas: the brainstorming technique can help.

Disagreement can lead either to hard feelings or to innovation, depending largely upon the sense of purpose, standards and atmosphere which you as the leader create in the group. Encourage the clash of ideas; discourage the clash of personalities.

The idea-generating process should be kept separate from the idea-evaluation process, because criticism tends to inhibit creativity.

Seek to develop a range of feasible choices or alternatives in the middle part of the discussion, keeping an open mind for sudden or later inspiration.

Remember that a solution propounded by you as the leader is likely to be improperly evaluated – the group tends to either accept or reject it. Make sure your ideas are submitted to the same disciplines as everyone else's.

If you are not part of the solution you are part of the problem.

13   Team maintenance

Work groups can be divided into temporary and permanent. A temporary or *ad hoc* team or group is formed for a specific purpose and then disbands when that is accomplished. 'Task forces' and project groups belong to this category. A permanent or standing team continues in existence, with gaps in membership made up by new recruits. Committees can belong to either category.

There are pros and cons to both types of work group. Most people respond well to having a limited commitment of time, like a sprinter who can clearly see the finishing tape. Against that, such groups often disband when they are just becoming real teams in the sense defined in this book.

The chief advantage of the permanent team is that members do come to know each other and each other's capabilities exceptionally well. They should be able to work more effectively together. But such groups can become cosy and comfortable, like an old pair of slippers. Even assuming that they are still fully effective, they need regular servicing and maintenance. Then they can perform at a level of excellence over a long period. Team maintenance in that sense is the subject of this chapter. How do you keep a good team in its existing state of efficiency and effectiveness?

MAINTAINING CORE PURPOSE

It is comparatively easy to select a core purpose, recruit a team and break the purpose down into manageable aims and objectives. It is much harder to maintain the core purpose of the team, committee or group over a length of time. As a leader you should be prepared from time to time to ask yourself and the team the following questions:

- Why do we exist, what are we here for?
- What and who would be affected if we went out of existence?
- Are there more cost-effective ways our purpose and aim could be achieved than having this team?
- Has there been a significant change in our mission as a team? Have we perceived – or been given – new responsibilities?
- Are we still the right people to be tackling this work? Does it still need a team effort?

Remember that groups have a tendency to want to perpetuate themselves. The instinct for survival comes into play. We are here because we are here. Any move to disband the group can be perceived as a threat to unity. The desire for self-perpetuation *regardless of task* has taken over. The group has become a family, not a team.

Therefore as leader you must reassure yourself (if not others) at intervals that there still is a real task for this group to perform and that it still requires the degree of teamwork you are seeking to build and maintain.

MAINTAINING STANDARDS

Standards, you recall, are the group norms – usually unwritten – which largely determine corporate behaviour of the group. There may be, for example, a high standard of attentiveness to each other in one group while in another you may notice that no one is listening to their neighbour or anyone else.

Standards are technical as well as interpersonal. Ideally groups should set themselves, with some direction from their leader, standards of performance which they think they can attain. These should be neither too high nor too low, but sufficiently stretching or challenging to grip interest and – when achieved – to pay a dividend in sense of achievement.

Over a period, however, two things can happen. First, the team's standards can slip. Idleness, indifference or that disease of success called complacency set in. These malaises introduce a general feeling of 'anything goes here'.

Secondly, the world outside the organisation changes. Standards in your given field or industry are constantly rising. What seemed to be high performance, high productivity or good sense to the customer ten years ago now seems mediocre judged from an impartial standpoint.

One first-aid remedy for declining standards is to generate a sense of competition. The fat and lazy manager entered for a marathon has some incentive to become lean and active. So it is with groups and organisations. The first step is for you as leader to bring home to the team that, good though its performance is, it is no longer good enough. 'Good enough for what?' asks the anxious team members. 'Good enough to beat the competition', you reply.

Competition, you recall, deals with relative positions on a league table. But the true end of competing with others is not the transitory pleasures of winning. The true end of striving against competitors is to raise your standards against some absolute scale of value. That goal is summed up by the word *excellence*. To compete means literally to seek something together. Actual competitions should be regarded as incentives, milestones, even games, but not the real object of the exercise.

It is not much good holding up absolute values like 'excellence' to a team with slipping standards. Your words will sound like 'motherhood' – abstract and banal. But tell the team or organisation where it stands in relation to the competition as factually as possible. Invite them to tell you why they are so low on the scale. Formulate with them some plans which will take you further up the ladder within a given time.

CASE STUDY

When Julian Pritchard became chief executive of Penleys Bank it was like taking over a national institution. Penleys had been established in 1762. The Penley family provided a notable line of bankers until after the 1974 oil crisis. In the ensuing more difficult economic conditions the Penleys and their friends on the board eventually found themselves presiding over declining profitability. For the first time the family bank, which prided itself on being a large family, had to declare redundancies. Pritchard was brought in from another more successful bank in 1984. 'Look', he told his executive committee of directors, 'we are in the middle of a revolution in the City of London, not to mention new competition from American and other foreign banks. At present Penleys is about third or fourth in the second division of merchant banks. My aim is to get it up into the first division within three years. That means that we have to raise our standards of technical performance, profitability and customer service. Could I have your views please?'

You can see what Pritchard is doing. He is using the language of the football league table to express in shorthand his resolve to transform the standards of Penleys Bank. In order to stand still, let alone to reach the top three places in the 'first division' of merchant banks, those standards have to be much higher. In the climate of modern banking, where tasks are increasingly complex and interrelated, that is going to require a higher quality of teamwork in Penleys between departments who have hitherto seen themselves in separate boxes. Standards of presentation to potential clients will have to go up; the aftercare services of the backroom technical and administrative staff need to be of a high order. It is vital that these people doing routine and relatively unexciting office functions feel themselves as much a part of the team as the 'star players' in Penleys corporate finance division. Julian Pritchard has a formidable leadership challenge in front of him. What do you think his next steps should be?

From this case study you can see why I prefer the term teambuilding to team maintenance. If a human group resembled a machine, perhaps maintenance – repair, replacing parts, oiling and greasing – would be the right word. You can maintain a machine or a house in its present state. But a leader is unlikely to be satisfied with any such present state. To repeat, you should never finish building your team. As a living entity it is either growing or fading, never standing still. To *maintain* standards you must aim for *higher* standards.

COPING WITH CONFLICT

What do you do if the team threatens to fall apart because there is personal conflict between two or more members? By conflict here I mean primarily a clash of personalities rather than ideas.

The first strategy is to attempt to de-personalise the issue so that the difference of ideas or policies becomes central. This is not easy because personalities and issues tend to become intertwined.

As a prelude to discussing conflict in this wider sense it may be useful to chart the ways the different individuals are responding to the fact of a conflict of ideas between them. They adopt one of the following behaviours outlined in Fig. 13.1.

Competition/Forcing Tries to force his own way/ideas through	Gets results; alright when quick concerted action is required. If idea/course of action is bad time is wasted; teamwork reduced; other views not heard.
Collaboration/Confronting Brings issues into the open in order to explore all feasible options. He will move all the way if convinced.	Quality of results is better; commitment of team is higher. May take a long time, and is frustrating for people looking for early decision.

Sharing/Compromise
He is willing to negotiate a half-way position, and is therefore prepared to move that far.

Everyone gets something; no one solution is preferred. May be only way to get a result. But the quality of the compromise solution or decision may be inferior and commitment to it poor.

Avoiding
He opts out when conflict arises, waiting for others to solve it; avoids taking up a position.

Reduces tension. May result in good ideas being lost. Usually leads to a shelving or postponement of the conflict, not its resolution.

Accommodation/Smoothing
He is worried about hurting other people's feelings by seeming to disagree with them. Leans over backwards to avoid giving offense or to repair 'the damage'.

On unimportant issues may be best way of maintaining group unity. Can seem patronising. Poor solutions often go through because of lack of challenge.

Fig. 13.1   Pros and Cons of Different Responses to Conflict

It can help individuals to see that they have fallen into one mode of handling conflicts of ideas and that there are other options open. It is good sometimes to experiment with a bolder style if you happen to be timid by nature, or a more compromising, open and accommodating approach if your natural tendency is to try to dominate 'the opposition' with your own ideas.

Returning to interpersonal or intergroup tension: it is a matter of judgement to decide at what point the tensions begin to turn into conflicts that will seriously impair the work of that team and which call for intervention. But you must, as a leader, be ready to make that judgement and then take appropriate action.

Should you decide that confronting conflict will lead to higher cohesiveness eventually, the next step to realise is that you do not hold all the cards – only half of them. If there is a conflict between A and B in your team it is going to be primarily those two people who resolve it – or it will simply fester and splutter on. You can help in various ways as mediator. You can bring some pressure on them: the various non-violent forms of 'knocking their heads together'. For example, you can set a time limit in which you want their differences to have been settled, suggesting a third party arbitrator to help. Or you can offer to act in the role of consultant, catalyst or change agent yourself to bring about reconciliation, although it may be difficult to combine that role with being leader and therefore ultimately accountable for the work of the team.

Culture plays a part in determining how far conflict involving strong emotions should be brought out into the open. In the American Group Dynamics tradition it was felt that all conflicts should be brought out into the open – by the trainer if by no one else – and worked through. Equally the expression of feelings, however negative or hostile, was encouraged for cathartic reasons. That American approach was introduced into teambuilding activities in other parts of the world. It is well illustrated in this further extract from Iain Mangham's case study 'Building an Effective Work Team'.

Resolving Conflict

The question of working-through rather than backing-off became very prominent when the members focused on the reactions to the question on conflict. The scores revealed that nearly all the members considered it useful to 'let sleeping dogs lie'. There appeared to be strong feelings that conflict must be avoided whatever the personal costs. The consultant invited the members to give free associations around the notion of conflict and a very impressive list of negative connotations was generated: 'violence', 'destruction', 'vicious', 'cruel', 'hurt', 'smash', 'batter', 'war', 'fight', 'bitter struggle', 'immature squabble', etc. The implications of this negativism were discussed and a handout on conflict was distributed to reinforce the points made by the consultants; conflict *could* be positive, issues *could* be worked through and resolved.

After some general conversation around the need for people to face up to problems, the consultant intervened:

'What does this discussion mean for this section here and now? What conflicts do we envisage in talking about the problems we have in working together?'

This intervention prompted an almost immediate return to the questionnaire. Gradually, however, an atmosphere of openness and trust was being established. The development of this was greatly facilitated by the attitude of the section manager who was willing, as he rather unfortunately put it, 'to stick my neck on the block'. At several points he intervened to suggest that his role be discussed.

'I'm willing to listen to any comments.'

Both he and the members realised how difficult it was to discuss roles and relationships even though the consultant gave them support and encouraged them to comment on each other's actions in an essentially non-evaluative fashion. They were encouraged to say, 'What you did made me feel such and such a feeling,' rather than bluntly saying, 'What you did was stupid, wrong, wicked, etc.' In the former manner it was stressed that the recipient was more likely to *hear* the comment, could test his intentions against the reality fed back to him by the respondent and could modify his future behaviour if he *chose to do so*.

Listening to what others said, of course, was bound up with how they presented what they had to say, but listening in itself was a central concern of the consultant's interventions. Members realised how little they listened when they were challenged by the consultant to repeat the other man's argument before they attempted to counter it. Such interventions led to a marked improvement in mutual attention, to an improvement in *really* hearing what the other had to say rather than seizing upon points on which he could be attacked.

Attention to the feelings or emotions of people in conflict situations pays dividends. But whether or not to encourage people to express their negative emotions towards each other, privately or in public, must always be a matter of judgement. For there is a calculated risk to be taken either way. Will it lead to improved relationships, or is the cure worse than the illness? A close scrutiny of the situation and personalities will usually tell you the right answer.

The ultimate resolution of conflict usually stems from the emotional discovery – or rediscovery – that we need each other if we are going to complete the common task. If both individuals or parties value that common task, albeit for different reasons, they will be willing to make the necessary sacrifices and adjustments. The advantages of co-operating to achieve results prove stronger than the displeasures of inter-necine warfare. If reasoning fails and the conflict worsens, you may have to make radical changes in the composition of the team.

To return to an earlier theme, you should help team members to distinguish between the ideas of a person and the person himself. Getting team members to see the good in each other – and to accept it while living with their private or open rejection of other parts of their colleague's personality – is part of the teaching function of leadership. It is an aspect of personal development, of growing together into maturity.

The ideal, of course, is to have a high level of mutual trust, respect and – if possible – affection between members of the team combined with a toughness towards each other's ideas. What should be central is the common quest for the truth of the matter. In that pursuit the blows may come thick and fast but they are not perceived or taken as being personal in any way, just as two professional boxers trade punches. Each member of the team has learnt how to accept the other person while rejecting his idea if it merits rejection.

THE CASE OF THE POOR PERFORMER

Dr Neutrino is a lecturer in the Department of Astronumeric Engineering. He has been in the University since his late twenties and is now fifty-three years old. He has done little or no research, except for two short papers ten years ago. His lecture course produces poor examination results. Final year degree students have commented that his notes and example sheets are insufficiently rigorous. His teaching style is barely adequate. His colleagues find Neutrino has become apathetic; he is unenterprising and unwilling to exert himself. He does not initiate any exchanges with the students, but is helpful when approached. He is frequently absent or late arriving. Despite all this he is likeable. His colleagues have been tolerant about his shortcomings for several years, but now the necessity for improving standards of the department is very real. For Astronumeric Engineering will suffer from the cut-backs in government funding, and some departments – the less good ones – will have to close in two years time; no one knows which ones. The last head of department had some rows with Neutrino but then gave up – partly because Neutrino hurt *his* feelings by what he said about the department and partly because he did not like rows. 'The University cannot sack Neutrino because he has security of job tenure', he explained to you when you took over as departmental head six months ago. But Neutrino's colleagues are getting more restive; three of them have been to talk to you about him privately in the last month. As leader of the team what are you going to do?

There is no short and simple answer to the case of the underachieving member in your team. The strategy for finding an answer, however, is plain.

First, you must *diagnose* the causes of underachievement. It may be lack of motivation, inadequate training, and poor leadership in the past. It may be that the person is in the wrong job – Neutrino should never have been a university lecturer. Still, as a leader you are like a golfer who has to play the ball where it lies.

If possible, check out your interpretation with the person concerned. He may add to, or subtract from, that picture of cause-and-effect you are trying to construct. Do not treat the symptoms, address the causes.

Ask Dr Neutrino what *he* wants – what motivates him now. He may want early retirement; if so you will be more than willing to help him achieve it. He may want to become a full member of the team but in a different role: perhaps more in an administrative capacity. List the *feasible options* for him and with him. But 'carrying on as we are now' is not allowed on the list!

An underachieving member may dispute the fact that he is so. Be prepared to tell him the impressions created by his behaviour in the department; what is observable to you and others – with some concrete examples in reserve to produce if necessary. This may lead into a discussion of Neutrino's attitudes. But you should avoid delving into his personality – positions central to the person – for that cannot be changed.

The end result should be an agreed action plan to restore the individual as a fully effective member of a team which is setting its sights and standards higher today than yesterday. That plan, like all plans, should be flexible. There should be a 'contract' with the person concerned to review progress at agreed intervals. The contingency option of parting company must always remain if that progress is not forthcoming.

CHECKLIST: DOES YOUR TEAM NEED MAINTENANCE

Does your team need maintenance? The following questions will help you to decide:

- Are there any symptoms of low morale, such as a decline in the team's self-confidence, a weakening of resolve and a loss of a sense of purpose?
- Has the group or organisation lost its sense of direction?
- Is each individual member still clear about the team's core mission and its principal aims? Are personal goals or objectives related to that purpose?
- Is the atmosphere of the group negative and lukewarm?
- Are individual members lacklustre in their enthusiasm?
- Has communication between members been dwindling?
- Are there signs of mistrust developing?
- All groups have potential 'metal fatigue' cracks. Are these cracks widening into divisions between individuals, cliques, or sub-groups?
- Have professional and personal standards declined in the last six months?
- Can you identify one or more individuals who are clearly underachieving when measured against today's group standards?
- Are there complaints about your leadership?

If you have answered *yes* to seven or more of these questions you need to maintain or build the team anew. Go back to the beginning of this chapter and re-read it carefully until an action plan begins to take shape in your mind.

POINTS TO PONDER

Teams, like friendships, need to be kept in good repair. Their purpose should be kept bright and burnished; their standards should be rising incrementally and their co-operation becoming ever closer and more effective.

You should encourage the clash of ideas, not personalities. There is enough conflict outside the organisation without fighting each other. Remember the African proverb: 'When the elephants fight it is the grass that gets trampled'.

Being on the same side should help you to develop hard debate in your group without the side effects of emotional hurt and interpersonal bitterness.

Never rest content with your team's level of performance. If they are *that* good they can be better tomorrow. Team maintenance is about removing those obstacles which prevent you growing as a team.

Do not be so busy on the common task that you forget the common life.

14 Roles revisited

In this chapter I shall comment briefly on some contemporary attempts at identifying unstructured roles in groups – the so-called team roles. Then, on the assumption that a business organisation is – or should be – a large team, I shall take a fresh look at some of the key roles that need to be clearly defined and fulfilled in an effective, flexible and creative way if an organisation wishes to enjoy sustained success.

A role is a capacity in which someone acts in relation to others. Roles can be structured to various degrees or relatively unstructured. My own inclination is to reserve the term for those relationships sufficiently structured in society or organisational life to have a common name and a set of expectations surrounding them.

The leader-follower roles fall somewhere in the middle of the structure-unstructured spectrum. They are more structured than many people imagine; less so than others believe. The matter is further complicated by the fact that the leader-follower roles never exist in a pure form: they are always associated with other much more structured roles (sales manager, colonel, bishop, hospital administrator, professor and so on).

TEAM ROLES

The attempt to give names to unstructured team roles is not new. Kenneth D. Benne and Paul Sheats couched their seminal work on functions in the language of personal roles in 1948 (see p. 40).

The following questions arise: if the leader does have his proper role in a team (as a guide, conductor, co-ordinator and so on), what is the proper role of a team member? Within that team member role, are there variations on the theme worthy to be called roles in their own right?

One study published in the mid-1970s suggested that there were a number of finite and limited roles 'adopted naturally by the various personality-types found among managers'. These 'team roles' were seven in number: Chairman, Plant (advancing new ideas), Monitor-Evaluator, Company Worker (translating ideas into practical working steps), Team Worker (supporting and helping others), Resource Investigator, and Completer. Much of the work was carried out by R.M. Belbin at Henley Management College over a period of seven years.[27]

In evaluating his approach, bear in mind that the groups studied were small discussion groups of managers participating in management courses. Therefore there is a distinctive situational dimension which has to be taken into serious account. Caution must therefore be exercised when it is claimed or implied that conclusions drawn from this type of study can be applied to teamwork in work situations.

Now we have already identified the *functions* necessary to achieve the task, to build or maintain the team, and to motivate, release and develop the contributions of each individual. The leader is accountable for these functions, though he should share and delegate them where possible. We have also reviewed the range of *mental processes* or abilities of the human mind, necessary or desirable when it comes to making decisions or solving problems or trying to think in new ways, such as analysing, synthesizing, valuing, imagining. And the point has been made that no one individual is likely to excel in all these kinds of mental contribution to group problem solving. It seems superfluous to add the notion that these functions/processes invariably cluster together in seven, eight or nine identifiable roles. Individuals will never conform to such types. One of the dangers of the listing of 'team roles' is that it does not adequately describe behaviour and can lead to stereotyping.

Surely the concept of role should not be allowed to become so loose and flexible as to be debased and meaningless. Individuals do indeed need to be encouraged to be able to spot and provide missing functions or thinking skills; they may indeed have natural proclivities towards one or two broad kinds of contribution rather than others. But it looks like little more than a party game to label them roles. To personify them as if they had some metaphysical existence is seriously misleading.

Despite the social-psychological tradition of attempting to identify and personify unstructured roles, I suggest that the key ingredients of roles in working groups are professional or technical: they involve degrees of specialisation and expertness. The performance of a team depends largely upon the individual member producing the goods according to their role and with the interests of the whole team in the forefront of their minds.

In the cricket or baseball analogy, some are more able and experienced batsmen and some are bowlers or pitchers. The latter, however, will find themselves in the role of batsmen. If a player is injured either may have to occupy the role of wicket keeper or catcher.

These team roles have a largely formal element in the sense that new members who perform a particular team role elsewhere can slot into the team immediately on arrival. Naturally their performance will improve when they have settled down in the team adjusting and eventually finetuning their ways of doing things with those of their colleagues.

Some teamwork throws up a particular role, that of a 'star performer'. Having such a person enables the group to achieve its purpose more effectively. But the 'star performer' ought to remain part of the team. If the 'star' sees himself as a merely outstanding performer within his role and widens praise bestowed on him to embrace the whole team, his prominence will not be resented. He will not become a *prima donna*.

A good example of a role structure of a team is a film crew, as shown opposite. Everyone has a specialist role but everyone has to work together as a team. Which would you identify as the leadership and management roles?

Role Call

Director
The film's creative force, but nowadays also expected to bring the picture in on time within the budget.

Producer
Ideally working tirelessly to find subjects and funding, then setting up and selling the film.

Associate producer
Is often the 'line producer', a vitally important role never, curiously, actually mentioned in the credits. The line producer is closely involved in the day-to-day running of the film. Goes with the crew on location, and has to be keenly aware of the financial implications of everything.

Cinematographer
Sometimes appears in the credits as 'Director of Photography'. Responsible for the way the film looks.

Camera operator
The person who actually controls the camera. A good operator will help the cinematographer and director get the shot they want – and tell them immediately when they have got it.

Focus puller
Responsible generally for looking after photographic equipment and specifically for keeping the camera in focus, with the right lens, and at the correct stop for the light.

Camera loader
Handles the clapperboard, loads film stock, and ensures there is enough film for each take.

Production designer
Finds, designs and builds the locations and sets which the cinematographer photographs. Works closely with the director, often providing him with sketches and ideas.

Editor
Spends many weeks closeted with the director in an editing suite, physically cutting and sticking together the film.

Assistant director
Indispensable and (ideally) indefatigable figure whose role on the set is organisational rather than artistic.

Second and third assistant directors
Work with the first assistant director, on mainly organisational duties – pushing extras about, briefing crowds.

Continuity
Ensures actor with patch over left eye in last scene is not wearing it over the right eye in the next. But also – more importantly – keeps a log of the whole production, checking the camera position and stop between scenes, keeping a running record of dialogue and taking photographs of every set.

Sound mixer
Records live sound, although some of the soundtrack may be 'looped' (recorded) later in the studio.

Boom operator
Holds the microphone for recording of live sound.

Dubbing mixer
Involved with the final edit of the film, mixing at least three soundtracks – dialogue, music and special effects – and often more.

Gaffer
Supervising electrician who works closely with cinematographer to achieve required lighting effects.

Best boy
The second electrician, working under the gaffer.

Art director
Works under the designer, ensuring that the sets conform to his designs. May also be given responsibility for designing specific sets.

Key grip
Responsible for moving the camera about, pushing it along for tracking shots and liaising with the other grips (or 'riggers') who build camera towers and tracking rails.

In summary, although I believe that there is a basic and positive role of follower or team member, I do not find the attempts to identify 'team roles' made by social psychologists in the least bit convincing. Each team member should have a different job, depending upon the nature of the work and the technology involved. Indeed it is sometimes useful to think of a team as primarily not a collection of persons but a tightly knit, interlocking and overlapping set of jobs. The proper names for these jobs, such as batsman or camera loader, describe the role the person is expected to play in the team.

In addition, an effective team member will contribute towards the three circles in a way that transcends his technical contribution. He or she, for example, will participate in making decisions or solving problems in a wider sense than merely offering specialist advice or criticism. He or she will also complement the work of the leader in helping to build the team and to meet individual needs. Such a person – technically skilled and socially competent – will fulfil the principal role of team member in a positive and inspiring way.

LINE AND STAFF ROLES

At management level there are essentially two kinds of jobs in organisations: line and staff. Line managers are responsible for results. They lead the teams which produce and market the goods or services at the right value for money. Staff managers are essentially advisory. They get results by helping line managers with specialist advice or technical knowledge.

Both roles require leadership. The line manager jobs – chief executive, manager, supervisor, chargehand-foreman-leading operative – have the three circles of task, team and individual as the core of their responsibilities, albeit at different levels of complexity. But senior staff managers – the head of personnel or the finance director – also have teams to be led in a similar way. In interacting with their colleagues, however, they must rely more upon the authority of knowledge – and persuasiveness – to get things done, rather than upon position-power.

One thing that can go wrong with the organisation as a team is for the wrong kinds of people to occupy these two roles. In teambuilding, you will recall, selecting the right person for the right job is an essential principle. Some people undoubtedly shine more in the line manager role than as staff or functional managers, and of course the reverse is true.

Creating a Management Team

Michael Edwardes moved from being Chief Executive and Chairman of Chloride to becoming Chairman of the ailing British Leyland in 1977. As part of his plan to restore management authority he set about reconstituting his management team, conscious of the different needs of line and staff appointments.

Another factor which persuaded me to follow instinct was that the psychological assessments of executives were showing a disturbing trend. The use of assessments as one factor in deciding on a person's suitability for a job is commonplace in the United States of America and among major international companies around the world. They were used extensively in Chloride, but the fact that I began to subject British Leyland executives to them, within days of arriving, gained widespread and usually fatuous publicity. Stories abounded of powerful and high-paid executives lying on couches or playing with bricks – the reality was nothing as fanciful, and had it been, we would have lost good men! What was required was just five hours of intense concentration at a desk. The tests are very demanding and they reveal a great deal about people's basic intellectual capacity as well as their style and approach to management tasks. My experience has been that their use in recruitment improves the success rate in making appointments on straight interviews from 50 per cent to approximately 90 per cent. The procedure reduces the failure rate; it doesn't eliminate error, but it is an invaluable aid to decision-making – even for internal deployment. Assessment is, of course, particularly useful in the case of recruitment when one is not familiar with the executives concerned. But the tests also gave a new opportunity to many existing managers in the company to slot into new and often more appropriate jobs. . .

We began to build up a picture of the strengths and weaknesses of our top 300 people, starting with the executive directors.

Of the top 300 managers, 60 were recruited externally by selective search plus psychological assessments, and although the remainder were found within the company, they had to be assessed and appraised because there was the need for extensive redeployment, and I could not be sure that internal appraisals were always objective. Of the other 240, no less than 150 managers found themselves in new positions, often because of the need to get 'line' people into 'managing' jobs and 'staff' people into basically advisory jobs. Too often there were staff men – excellent men – getting nowhere in jobs that required tough line types. Over the first months

> a few managers left the company of their own accord, but many more were asked to leave. In most cases we allowed the manager to 'resign' but in truth most of these people were dismissed, and were paid termination payments. We helped them to keep their reputations intact by inviting them to resign. Many were good men, but changes were needed; some had lost credibility, often through no fault of their own, others had been over-promoted and needed to start again elsewhere.

Line (of command) and staff are originally military terms – like strategy – which have been incorporated into general thinking about organisations. Military history abounds with examples of how a breakdown between commanders and staff officers can jeopardise the success of campaigns.

The more flexibility between the line and staff roles the individual manager can build into himself the more likely he is to find a route up to the summit of the mountain. He may find a resting place – not perhaps the right phrase! – somewhere short of that summit, but at least his decision will be based upon a realistic knowledge of his strengths and weaknesses – as revealed by experience, not by resort to personality tests.

RESPONSIBILITY CHARTING

Roles come to us rough-hewn. Business managers have a rough idea of named roles; for example, of Chairman, Managing Director or Non-Executive Director. Experience, discussion and reading can clarify these roles. This is valuable because all too often people occupying such roles have an impoverished concept of the role. Hence they tend to drag a job down to their level, rather than growing up into the job.

Even where you think you know what your role is, however, it is worth checking with your superior, colleagues and subordinates. There are different degrees of formality or structure for doing that, ranging from a conversation over lunch to an exchange of formal job descriptions. If roles are not so defined and agreed there can be trouble later. Consider these three short cases from my own experience as a consultant:

- Helen Hayward is the matron or chief nursing officer of a 120 bed hospital in the private sector. She is a good leader, setting clear objectives and high standards, building an exceptional team spirit among the staff – nurses, auxiliary and consultants – and taking time to develop each person. She enjoys her managerial responsibilities for her own budget and resources, and plans to move eventually more into administration. The Nonsuch Group, for whom she works, has expanded recently and appointed regional managers. The northern manager, Chris Keswick, is 32 years old, ten years younger than Helen, a thrusting, aggressive and successful executive. 'He has begun to interfere with my budget', says Helen. 'He holds meetings with my staff. I just don't have the freedom I used to have. It is all annoying and frustrating'.

- When David Roberts was appointed Bishop of Tenbury Wells he soon found that the Diocesan Secretary, a retired Army colonel called Henry Briggs, was really running the show. Briggs knew everyone – he had been there for fifteen years – and encouraged everyone to bring their problems to his office. No decisions were taken without consulting Briggs. At their first meeting Briggs suggested that David Roberts should devote himself to prayer, social activities and reading, leaving him to continue to run the diocese. The last straw came when the new Bishop found Briggs in his secretary's room going through the diary with her and telling her in future not to book dates for the Bishop without consulting him. 'Look Henry', said the Bishop, 'this cannot go on. We must sort out our roles'.

- Sir John Adams, a distinguished former chairman and chief executive of a large nationalised industry, was appointed non-executive chairman of a medium-sized firm making tiles for the building industry. Peter Beech, the managing director, had in effect been both chief executive and chairman before the arrival of Adams; he believes ardently that the two roles should be combined anyway. The board disagreed, not least because they thought Beech – a dynamic, 'hands on' leader – was far too immersed in the day-to-day running of the company. There was a lack of strategic thinking about new markets and overseas opportunities. 'Now I have got a chairman who will be breathing down my neck', Beech told his wife. 'There is enough stress in the job already without adding that one'.

In all these cases working relationships were improved when those involved submitted to each other their own job descriptions and their expectations of the other. Discrepancies were then discussed and ironed out. People had a high degree of commitment to the common task and a basic respect for the complementary contribution of the other person, so an accommodation was not difficult to reach.

Clarity over role is especially important in organisations which, although not matrixes in the full technical sense, have moved towards operating on the matrix principle.

What is a matrix?

The identifying feature of a matrix organisation is that some managers report to two bosses rather than to the traditional single boss; there is a dual rather than a single chain of command.

Companies tend to turn to matrix forms:

1 when it is absolutely essential that they be highly responsive to two sectors simultaneously, such as markets and technology;
2 when they face uncertainties that generate very high information processing requirements; and
3 when they must deal with strong constraints on financial and/or human resources.

Matrix structures can help provide both flexibility and balanced decision making, but at the price of complexity.

Matrix organisation is more than a matrix structure. It must be reinforced by matrix systems such as dual control and evaluation systems, by leaders who operate comfortably with lateral decision making, and by a culture that can negotiate open conflict and a balance of power.

In most matrix organisations there are dual command responsibilities assigned to functional departments (marketing, production, engineering, and so forth) and to product or market departments. The former are oriented to specialised in-house resources while the latter focus on outputs. Other matrices are split between area-based departments and either products or functions.

Every matrix contains three unique and critical roles; the top manager who heads up and balances the dual chains of command, the matrix bosses (functional, product, or area) who share subordinates, and the managers who report to two different matrix bosses. Each of these roles has its special requirements.

Aerospace companies were the first to adopt the matrix form, but now companies in many industries (chemical, banking, insurance, packaged goods, electronics, computer, and so forth) and in different fields (hospitals, government agencies, and professional organisations) are adapting different forms of the matrix.

From Stanley M. Davis and Paul R. Lawrence, 'Problems of Matrix Organisations', *Harvard Business Review*, May-June 1978

ON CLARIFYING ROLES

First, in thinking about a job you should try to separate the person and the personal attributes necessary for a job from the role and its decision making and communicating content, (but which taken together form the total picture of a person doing a job). You decide what sort of role you want to establish to get some work done and thereafter you find a person with the skills and personal attributes to fill that role appropriately for doing the work.

Secondly, when clarifying an old role or establishing a new one it is wise to consider it in two parts: (1) the definition of the nature and level of the decisions to be taken by it, and (2) the definition of the communicating relationship of the role with other roles in the organisation's accountability structure. Communication, here, is concerned with the status of what the role occupant is commissioned to say about a subject, whether it be instructions, advice, information, request, prescription or veto.

By now it should be possible – with a particular kind of key decision or activity (for example, form budget, allocate resources, select staff) – to be clear who has a part in that activity along the lines of the following classification:

- Responsibility for ensuring that decisions or actions occur.
- *Must* approve the decision, power of veto.
- *Must* be consulted but need not approve.
- *Must* be informed, but need not be consulted.
- *Must* support by provision of service or resource.

Whilst the quality of performance by the person in carrying out tasks and meeting targets will depend upon that person's skills and personality, by defining the role you have ensured that their potential for success, and hence the organisation's potential for success, has been enhanced. You can go ahead and agree targets – specific achievements to be required by certain dates.

This is not to say that all persons in an organisation must be forced into a straitjacket in which individuality ceases to exist.

Each person has his own style and flair which he can bring to a role and which interact with the style and flair of others in theirs. Properly drawn up and worded, a role or job description will provide wide freedom of action and opportunity for personal expression. It can result in a general release of personal creativity and talents which are sometimes locked away. When people are *not* clear about the limits of their accountability they tend to 'play safe' and cramp themselves within what they guess the limits to be, whereas when the limits are known the confidence thus generated sees them exploited to the full.

Working on the principle the roles should not be allowed to proliferate, it has been suggested that the basic types of roles in a business organisation can be reduced to seven:

Director	Responsible for the overall direction and condition of the organisation. Now a role performed as a team by a managing director with executive and non-executive directors on the board. (Note: the role of the latter often needs specifying.)
Manager	Fully accountable for the performance and results of all those who are subordinate to him. Within defined policies he is accountable for selecting, discharging, disciplining, training, promoting and paying his people.
Supervisor	Directly accountable for managing a group of non-managers, for example, operatives or clerks. Often responsible for seeing that a wide variety of detail is co-ordinated effectively. Does much of manager's lower-level managerial work with his authority, but is not thereby the operative's manager as manager retains for himself the basic decisions which are intrinsic to his role. The supervisor co-ordinates the subordinates, sees to their immediate needs and reports to the manager on performance.
Operative	Does directly productive work.
Leading operative	This person is doing productive work but is neither managerial nor supervisory. May be called a leading hand or charge hand or

	foreman. His own example directly influences the work output of the rest of the group.
Technical assistant	Saves the manager's time on matters that benefit from a specialised skill, for example, personal secretary. Does not involve the person in any decision making in connection with the manager's other subordinates.
Staff officer	As discussed already, the staff role is complementary to the role of line manager. Some of the work calls for specialised knowledge. In order to co-ordinate work in this sphere, the manager (or director) has a specialist to help him.

The relation of 'staff officer' and manager at senior level needs further exploration. In so far as he is doing the manager's work he should be regarded by all as a manager, but only strictly within the specialised sphere that his manager has made known to all. He and his manager must therefore at all times maintain a complete identity of view on all matters within his specialised sphere. To the extent that they differ, his line manager's views must prevail. Any differences of opinion between them are best kept between themselves. So instructions given by such a staff officer to his manager's subordinates ought to carry the authority of his manager.

Organisations are potentially large teams, then, because they comprise complementary roles based upon the principle of division of labour. Success depends upon each person fulfilling his or her role in harmony with the contributions of others, producing a result that no individual could achieve on his own. Leaders are needed to give a sense of direction, create a sense of teamwork, and to enable individuals to grow professionally and personally in their work. Even bureaucracies can respond to such leadership, as *The Times* (22.5.85) reported:

Lord Carrington, as he freely admits, is a man without power. As Secretary-General of Nato, he claims only to have influence. But it is a very powerful influence.

For those who work there his presence pervades and brightens the drab corridors of the Brussels headquarters. Ten months after taking office, the honeymoon period continues and it is difficult to find anyone with a bad word to say about him.

His arrival last June was like a breath of fresh air. Morale within Nato itself was not high, partly due to the way his predecessor worked. Dr Joseph Luns operated almost in isolation from the rest of the secretariat, relying mainly on his private office. There was no playback between the crew and the captain, and the crew seemed not entirely sure of where the ship was going.

From the moment he arrived, Lord Carrington set about bringing everyone into what was going on. Memos began moving back and forth, up and down the command structure. He would start an inquiry and send back his thanks – or criticisms – when the answer came. A sense of teamwork and personal involvement began to creep in. Voluntary overtime became more and more frequent.

Is it time that a sense of teamwork began to grow in your organisation?

POINTS TO PONDER

Beware of placing people into categories and labelling them as roles, for this can lead to stereotyping. The roles that people occupy in teams are based primarily upon their knowledge and skills, not their personalities. Beyond that, each of them should be good in the general role of team member. Some will be equipped for the role of leader.

Roles should fit together in an organisation, as in a team, like pieces of a jigsaw puzzle. Keep the pieces and the puzzle as simple as possible.

Clear role or job specifications for all members of the team or organisation – line managers or functional specialists, managing director or supervisor – are essential. They should not be detailed. Overlaps are inevitable and not undesirable.

Individualists, those who bring necessary creativity and flair to work groups, should learn to contribute through their role and not regardless of it. For vocation should be the servant of role, not its master. The secret of life is not to do what you like, but to like what you do.

When roles march in step the music is called team spirit: all for one and one for all.

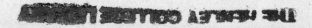

15 A checklist for team leaders

I have emphasised the role of the leader in teambuilding. In this last chapter I want to instil the desire to become more effective in that role. For the more skilled you become as a leader, the more rewarding you will find it to be. Enjoyment increases and the burden lightens.

There are a growing number of courses on leadership skills, both public ones – such as Action Centred Leadership (ACL) – and 'in-company' ones, in larger organisations at any rate. These can help you to develop your own leadership and team membership skills, especially if you attend them at the right time in your career: just before or shortly after taking up a leadership role.

But others cannot teach you leadership – you must learn it yourself. Establish your own strengths and weaknesses as a leader with ruthless objectivity. Then set to work over a reasonable time span. Remember that any self-development worthy of the name takes a considerable stretch of time, so start young if you can. Just as no man is born wise or learned so none is born a leader. Confidence is a plant of slow growth.

The following checklist is designed to help you apply the principles of this book to your team now. Doing things differently, making improvements there, can be the first steps on your much longer road of self-development as a leader. An inch is a cinch, a yard is hard.

Do not be afraid of making mistakes on that journey. Failures teach success. They also teach humility.

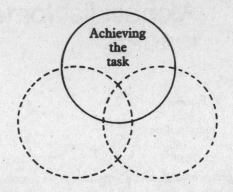

TASK:

Purpose:	Am I clear what the task is?
Responsibilities:	Am I clear what mine are?
Objectives:	Have I agreed these with my superior, the person accountable for the group?
Programme:	Have I worked one out to reach objectives?
Working conditions:	Are these right for the job?
Resources:	Are these adequate (authority, money, materials)?
Targets:	Has each member clearly defined and agreed them?
Authority:	Is the line of authority clear? (Accountability chart)?
Training:	Are there any gaps in the specialist skills or abilities of individuals in the group required for the task?
Priorities:	Have I planned the time?
Progress:	Do I check this regularly and evaluate?
Supervision:	In case of my absence who covers for me?
Example:	Do I set standards by my behaviour?

NOTES:

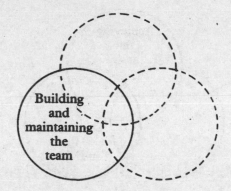

TEAM MEMBERS:

Objectives: Does the team clearly understand and accept them?

Standards: Do they know what standards of performance are expected?

Safety standards: Do they know consequences of infringement?

Size of team: Is the size correct?

Team members: Are the right people working together? Is there a need for subgroups to be constituted?

Team spirit: Do I look for opportunities for building teamwork into jobs? Do methods of pay and bonus help to develop team spirit?

Discipline: Are the rules seen to be reasonable? Am I fair and impartial in enforcing them?

Grievances: Are grievances dealt with promptly? Do I take action on matters likely to disrupt the group?

Consultation: Is this genuine? Do I encourage and welcome ideas and suggestions?

Briefing: Is this regular? Does it cover current plans, progress and future developments?

Represent: Am I prepared to represent the feelings of the group when required?

Support: Do I visit people at their work when the team is apart? Do I then represent to the individual the whole team in my manner and encouragement?

NOTES:

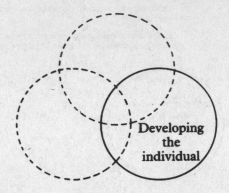

INDIVIDUAL:

Targets:	Have they been agreed and quantified?
Induction:	Does s/he really know the other team members and the organisation?
Achievement:	Does s/he know how his/her work contributes to the overall result?
Responsibilities:	Has s/he got a clear and accurate job description? Can I delegate more to him/her?
Authority:	Does s/he have sufficient authority for his/her task?
Training:	Has adequate provision been made for training or retraining both technical and as team member?
Recognition:	Do I emphasise people's successes? In failure is criticism constructive?
Growth:	Does s/he see the chance of development? Does s/he see some pattern of career?
Performance:	Is this regularly reviewed?
Reward:	Are work, capacity and pay in balance?
The task:	Is s/he in the right job? Has s/he the necessary resources?
The person:	Do I know this person well? What makes him/her different from others?
Time/attention:	Do I spend enough with individuals listening, developing, counselling?
Grievances:	Are these dealt with promptly?

| *Security:* | Does s/he know about pensions, redundancy and so on? |
| *Appraisal:* | Is the overall performance of each individual regularly reviewed in face-to-face discussion? |

NOTES:

Conclusion

I have emphasised the role of the leader in teambuilding. It is essential for organisations to develop individuals who are skilled at building and maintaining teams. I have assumed that you are such a leader – potential or actual. Lastly, I have suggested that, if you are trained to lead, it will help you be more effective when you are working in the role of a team member. For most managers wear at least two hats: leader and team member. The ideal is to reach excellence in both roles.

In temporary or *ad hoc* groups an important part of your role as leader will be to manage the interface between the team and its sponsors and clients, transmitting their messages to the team. It is a two-way traffic: you also need to secure the necessary outside resources for the team. Directing (setting aims and objectives), facilitating the interdependent contributions of members as a team, relating to each individual member in a positive constructive way; these are the essentials of the role of leader.

Example is all-important in teambuilding. It is not an easy path. Most of us can echo Shakespeare's words in *The Merchant of Venice*:

> I can easier teach twenty what were good to be done, than to be one of the twenty to follow my own teaching

As a leader you have to embody truth, not theorise about it.

The role of team member is positive. Its very lack of structure invites you to be creative in it: more like playing jazz music extempore than following a composer's score.

Active attentiveness, building on ideas, testing ideas with criticism, making suggestions; all these are manifestations of someone who sees team membership in this positive and constructive light. In other situations you may be the appointed or elected leader but here you have 'contracted' to serve as a team member. That means you will behave in a certain way. You will make your views known, but will loyally accept the 'lawful authority' of the leader and actively support him. You can, for example, complement him by supplying missing functions in the task, team or individual areas. For the perfect leader does not exist. Your leader will have weaknesses. See them as opportunities for helping, not occasions for carping to colleagues. Good team members can make poor leaders look good, and better leaders look excellent. It is a creative role in that sense as well.

Individualists, as opposed to individual persons, will find these skills much harder to acquire and practise. Having a strong preference for doing things your way makes it difficult to work within the constraints of a team effort. Of course it depends upon how strong your bias towards individualism proves to be. Not all individualists are loners. Individual specialists of outstanding ability may often be difficult to work with but it is a price both leader and the rest of the team are prepared to pay in return for their gifts. The challenge is to create an atmosphere in which those gifts can flourish, and also where they can learn to co-operate with others and produce their best. In time the 'prima donna' may come to see that he or she is powerless without the 'full supporting cast' of the team, and modesty – living within one's true limits – may begin to dawn.

We often picture a team as a number of people running around on a playing field, working together in one place or sitting around a table making decisions.

Yet team work is equally important when the team is physically dispersed. Much of the work of teams or organisations is done by individuals working on their own.

Such team members need vision or imagination if they are to work as a team even when they are apart. They need to see the whole, for instance the end product as experienced by the customer or client. For the latter are often receiving pieces of teamwork in a serial fashion. First, metaphorically, the electricians wire up the room and then the plasterers arrive. It soon becomes apparent *to the customer* whether the building firm (or its equivalent) is working as an effective team or as merely a collection of individuals fulfilling roles, individuals or groups out of touch – often out of sympathy – with each other or with other groups in the same organisation.

The complexities of modern organisations, especially those which operate consciously or unconsciously on the matrix principle, lead inevitably to role conflicts. The electrician may want to wire your house, but he belongs also to another team working on the brewery down the road and he is wanted there. Who has the prior claim on his services? Who decides?

Teams need to develop common standards that they will adhere to while working apart. These will be in addition to the professional, technical or craftsmanship standards inculcated by vocational training. They include standards about communication with each other as well as the team spirit of service to the customer. Creating this climate or atmosphere, establishing common ways of doing things, that is your responsibility as leader, although you would be wise to enlist all the help you can get. Let your influence travel with each team member.

The need for such teamwork in order to raise quality of performance is growing more pressing. The Office of Fair Trading in Britain reported in 1985 that some eighteen million people – more than 40 per cent of the adult population – are dissatisfied with goods bought or services paid for. Therefore there is certainly no room for complacency in shops and stores, the service industries or manufacturing industry. The time is ripe to make a quantum leap forward in the way that people work together in industry and commerce.

If you are a competent leader and a person of professional and personal integrity, a leader who has won the respect of those that work for him and besides him, people will say this about you:

- he is 'human' and treats us as human beings

- he has no favourites; he doesn't bear grudges

- it is easy to talk to him – he listens and you can tell he listens

- he keeps his word and he is honest

- he doesn't dodge unpleasant issues

- he explains why – or else why not

- he's fair with his praise as well as his criticisms and he criticises without making an enemy of you
- he is fair to us as well as the company
- he drives himself hard so you don't mind him expecting the best of you

You will be getting the required results, your group will be working purposefully as a team, and each individual feels he is playing a vital part in the success of the group. The three circles then begin to take shape:

A guide to resources

BOOKS

The reference list below is by no means exhaustive, but is designed to provide a broad introduction to the fields of leadership, teambuilding and organisation.

Adair, J., *Action-Centred Leadership*, Gower, 1979.
Adair, J., *Effective Leadership*, Gower, and Pan, 1983.
Adair, J., *Skills of Leadership*, Gower, 1984.
Adair, J., *Management Decision Making*, Gower, 1984, and Pan, 1985 under the title *Effective Decision-Making*.
Belbin, R.M., *Management Teams: Why They Succeed or Fail*, Heinemann, 1981.
Bonner, K., *Group Dynamics: Principles and Application*, New York, Ronald Press, 1959.
Cribbin, J.J., *Effective Managerial Leadership*, American Management Association, New York, 1972.
Douglas, T., *Basic Groupwork*, Tavistock, 1978.
Douglas, T., *Groups: Understanding People Gathered Together*, Tavistock, 1983.
Drucker, P.F., *The Effective Executive*, Pan, 1970.
Dyer, W.G., *Team Building: Issues and Alternatives*, Addison-Wesley, 1977.
Graham, H.T., *Human Resources Management*, Macdonald and Evans Handbooks, 1979.
Handy, C., *Understanding Organisations*, Penguin, 1976.
Hunt, J., *Managing People at Work*, Pan, 1981.
Mackenzie, Davey D. and Harris, M., *Judging People*, McGraw Hill, 1982.
Mant, A., *Leaders We Deserve*, Martin Robertson, 1983.

Merry, U. and Allerhand, M.E., *Developing Teams and Organisations: A Practical Handbook for Managers and Consultants*, Addison-Wesley, 1977.

Oldcorn, R., *Management: A Fresh Approach*, Pan, 1982.

Phillips, K. and Fraser, T., *The Management of Interpersonal Skills Training*, Gower, 1982.

Stewart, R., *The Reality of Management*, Pan, 1963 (revised edition, 1985).

Woodcock, M., *Team Development Manual*, Gower, 1979.

Woodcock, M. and Francis, D., *Organisation Development through Teambuilding*, Gower, 1981.

For more general information on working in groups, the following may be helpful:

Argyle, M., *The Social Psychology of Work*, Pelican, 1972.

Argyle, M., *The Psychology of Interpersonal Behaviour*, Pelican, 1967.

Brown, J.A.C., *The Social Psychology of Industry*, Pelican, 1971.

Cartwright, A. and Zander, A., *Group Dynamics*, Tavistock, 1960.

Schein, E.H., *Organisational Psychology*, Prentice-Hall, 1965.

Sprott, W.J.H., *Human Groups*, Pelican, 1958.

Sydney, E., Argyle, M. and Brown, M., *Skills with People*, Hutchinson, 1973.

TRAINING HANDBOOK SERIES

A Handbook of Management Training Exercises, Volume One, (1982), John Adair, Richard Ayres, Ian Debenham and David Despres.
Contains 25 loose-leaf exercises, covering a wide range of management skills, including: Communication, Creative Thinking, Group Working, Interpersonal Skills, Leadership and Team Building, Negotiating and Problem Solving.

A Handbook of Management Training Exercises, Volume Two, John Adair and David Despres.
Contains a further 28 exercises.

Training for Leadership: A Tutor's Manual, (1985), John Adair.
Consisting of ten sessions with supporting training

materials, the manual covers: Achieving the Task, Building the Team, and Developing the Individual.

Training for Decisions: A Tutor's Manual, (1976), John Adair.
This manual is designed to enable trainer training officers to conduct courses on decision making, problem solving and creative thinking, either as one-, two-, or three-day activities in their own right, or integrated into larger programmes of management or supervisory training.

Training for Communication: A Trainer's Manual, (1985), John Adair and David Despres.
The purpose of this trainer's manual is to help in the design and running of effective courses in the field of communication. The manual focuses upon the personal skills of communication: speaking – the principles and practice of public speaking, listening – the attitudes and skills of a good listener, writing – sharpening letter writing and report writing skills, reading – both faster and more comprehensive reading, interviewing – the conduct of effective appraisal interviews, meetings – the art of chairing committees and meetings.

These training handbooks are all available from BACIE (The British Association for Commercial and Industrial Education), 16 Park Crescent, London W1N 4AP

References

1 For a discussion of various training methods stemming from the Group Dynamics movement, see *Training in Small Groups*, ed. B. Babington Smith and B.A. Farrell, Pergamon, 1979.

2 Edgar, H. Schein, *Organisational Psychology*, second edition, Prentice-Hall, 1970.

3 Bernard M. Bass, *Leadership, Psychology and Organisational Behaviour*, Harper and Row, 1960.

4 T. Douglas, *Groups*, Tavistock, 1983.

5 N. Hamilton, *Monty: The Making of a General*, Hamish Hamilton, 1981.

6 Matthew B. Miles, *Learning to Work in Groups*, Columbia University, 1959.

7 See for instance, H. Bonner, *Group Dynamics: Principles and Applications*, Ronald Press, 1959.

8 See T. Douglas, *Basic Group Work*, Tavistock, 1978 and *Groups*, Tavistock, 1983.

9 'Functional roles of group members', *Journal of Social Issues*, Vol. 4, No. 2 (1948), pp. 41-49.

10 See H. Bonner, *op. cit*, Part 4, 'The Person in the Group'.

11 G.C. Homans, *Social Behaviour: Its Elementary Forms*, New York, Harcourt, Brace, 1961.

12 See Chapter 4, 'The Individual'. For further study: A. Harblaster, *The Rise of Western Liberalism*.

13 Francis Quarles (1592-1644), *Esther*, Sec. 1, Meditation 1.

14 J.R. Gibb and L.M. Gibb, *Applied Group Dynamics*, National Training Laboratories, 1955. The first composite list of functions, reflecting 'task orientation' and 'socio-emotional orientation', in the T-Group context, was produced by R.F. Bales, *Interaction Process Analysis: A*

Method for the Study of Small Groups, Addison-Wesley, 1950.

15 In this section I follow closely the argument of Antony Flew, 'Competition and Co-operation, Equality and Elites', *Journal of Philosophy of Education*, Vol. 17 (1983).

16 *Training in Small Groups, op. cit.*, pp. 117-18.

17 M. Argyle, *The Social Psychology of Work*, Penguin, 1972.

18 Published by Routledge and Kegan Paul.

19 *Basic Groupwork*, Tavistock, 1978.

20 G.M. material from D. Clutterbuck, 'General Motors strives to motivate its workers', *International Management*, Jan. 1975.

21 *Management Education and Development*, Vol. 15, pt. 2 (1984), pp. 163-175.

22 *Group Training Techniques*, Gower, 1972.

23 See my *Management Decision Making*, Gower, 1985.

24 Alex F. Osborn, *Applied Imagination*, revised edition, New York, Charles Scribner, 1957.

25 See G.M. Prince, *The Practice of Creativity*, Harper & Row (1970) for an account of a group tackling this particular problem.

26 N.F.R. Maier, 'Assets and Liabilities in Group Problem Solving', Psychological Review, Vol. 74 No. 4 (1967). See also his book *Problem Solving Discussions and Conferences*, Wiley, 1963.

27 R.M. Belbin, *Management Teams: Why They Succeed or Fail*, Heinemann, 1981. Nine different roles are suggested by C.J. Margerison in *Managing Effective Work Groups*, McGraw-Hill, 1973. These are: Reporter, Creator, Explorer, Assessor, Thruster, Producer, Controller, Upholder and Linker. D. Krech and R. Crutchfield, "*Theory and Problems in Social Psychology*, McGraw-Hill, 1948, suggested yet another list: Group Representative, Controller of internal relationships, Purveyor (of rewards and punishments), Arbitrator, Exemplar, Group Symbol, Surrogate (for individual responsibility), Father figure, Scapegoat.

Index

John Adair

Effective Leadership
How to develop leadership skills

The art of good leadership is highly prized and demands a keen ability to appraise, understand and inspire both colleagues and subordinates.

Effective Leadership is carefully structured to ensure a steady, easily acquired insight into leadership skills, helping you to:
• understand leadership – what you have to be, know and do
• develop leadership abilities – defining the task, planning, briefing, controlling and setting an example
• grow as a leader – making certain your organization encourages leaders to emerge

John Adair, Britain's foremost expert on leadership training, shows how every manager can learn to lead. He draws upon numerous examples of leadership in action – commercial, historical, military – all pinpointing the essential requirements.

The ideal passport to the development of leadership.

John Adair

Effective Innovation
How to stay ahead of the competition

Innovation – the process of taking new ideas through to satisfied customers – is the lifeblood of any organization today. Nothing stultifies a company and the individuals working in it more than a lack of interest in positive change. You cannot stand still: either you go backwards or move forwards.

In *Effective Innovation* John Adair looks at both creativity and innovation: generating new ideas and bringing them to market. His 'seven habits of successful creative thinkers' provides a compelling framework for developing your own productive thinking skills. This readable book also covers leadership of creative teams and discusses how to build an innovative climate in organizations.

A complete guide to a core management competence.

John Adair

Effective Innovation
How to stay ahead of the competition

John Adair

Effective Motivation
How to get extraordinary results from everyone

People are the most important asset in any business today. Great results
come from great people. Every manager needs to be able to motivate or
draw out the best from others, which is not easy in times of corporate
change and personal uncertainty.

Effective Motivation is a practical guide to this key leadership skill.
Based on a careful evaluation of the research into motivation, John
Adair presents a set of strategies for motivating high-performance
teams and individuals. Case studies, checklists and exercises help the
reader to put the principles behind motivation to productive use.

All Pan Books are available at your local bookshop or newsagent, or can be ordered direct from the publisher. Indicate the number of copies required and fill in the form below.

Send to: Macmillan General Books C.S.
              Book Service By Post
              PO Box 29, Douglas I-O-M
              IM99 1BQ

or phone: 01624 675137, quoting title, author and credit card number.

or fax: 01624 670923, quoting title, author, and credit card number.

or Internet: http://www.bookpost.co.uk

Please enclose a remittance* to the value of the cover price plus 75 pence per book for post and packing. Overseas customers please allow £1.00 per copy for post and packing.

*Payment may be made in sterling by UK personal cheque, Eurocheque, postal order, sterling draft or international money order, made payable to Book Service By Post.

Alternatively by Access/Visa/MasterCard

Card No.

Expiry Date

Signature

Applicable only in the UK and BFPO addresses.

While every effort is made to keep prices low, it is sometimes necessary to increase prices at short notice. Pan Books reserve the right to show on covers and charge new retail prices which may differ from those advertised in the text or elsewhere.

NAME AND ADDRESS IN BLOCK CAPITAL LETTERS PLEASE

Name

Address

8/95

Please allow 28 days for delivery.
Please tick box if you do not wish to receive any additional information. ☐